Walking Tall

Walking Tall

Healing from domestic violence, abuse and trauma.

Calli J. Linwood

Unless otherwise indicated, all Scripture is from the New Living Translation. (NLT)

All journal entries and appendix articles are taken directly, as they were written, from the author's personal journal. All names have been changed to protect the privacy of the individuals.

ISBN# 978-1-988001-06-7

Published by Ahelia Publishing, Inc.
Printed in the United States of America
www.aheliapublishing.com
aheliapublishing@outlook.com
www.facebook.com/aheliapublishing

To Contact Calli directly, please email her at Cjlinwood@outlook.com

AHELIA PUBLISHING, INC.

The purpose of this book is to bring the darkness of domestic violence into the light, and to give a voice to the plight of the voiceless ones.

I am the LORD your God, who brought you out of the land of Egypt so you would no longer be their slaves. I broke the yoke of slavery from your neck so you can walk with your heads held high.

Leviticus 26:13

*T*he orchards and fields of my people will yield bumper crops, and everyone will live in safety. When I have broken their chains of slavery and rescued them from those who enslaved them, then they will know that I am the LORD. They will no longer be prey for other nations, and wild animals will no longer devour them. They will live in safety, and no one will frighten them.

Ezekiel 34:27-30

A Note From the Author

I do not write the ugly stuff to sensationalize it. It was not sensational. I do not write the ugly stuff to glorify it. It was not glorious. I do write the ugly stuff to show you where I came from and what I walked through. I do write the ugly stuff to magnify how amazing it is that I am now where I am ... the fact that I am walking tall with my Savior, totally changed, totally free, and at peace ... **That** is sensational. **That** is glorious.

My mom used to say, "I thought you'd be much worse for much longer." That is a testament to the new creation I have become. I was not just put back together, but have been recreated in the image of Christ, by following the healing steps He so carefully laid out in my life. Though all the events in this book are true, the timeline is fuzzy. It is not a chronological account of my life, nor is it supposed to be. Rather, it contains little packets of healing, which I pray will help the reader reflect on her own journey, question things in her own life, and find her own road to healing, continual freedom, and infinite blessing.

I chose not to use names, or to change the ones I did use. I want to honor and respect the privacy of all those involved. I left my children out of it as much as was possible. That is not my story to tell--it is theirs. Maybe, one day, they will tell it.

May God bless you.
Love in Christ,
Calli

CONTENTS

Contents Cont'd . . .

Part 3 – Now What?

It was a Tuesday in June of 2015, when I was at a Gospel Camp, on the prairies of Saskatchewan. I had not been back to camp since I was a counselor there, 25 years previous, but God undoubtedly called me back that summer. Even though I had to drive my son into the city to attend a birthday party that afternoon, I knew I had to be back for the church service that evening. I rushed back to camp, walking into the service over an hour late. As I responded to the altar call, Pastor Jay Pike, from Oklahoma, prayed over me and began to prophesy.

"I see barbs in your heart, like many, many wounds, and God is saying that He is coming to heal them with the balm of Gilead. You are going into a new season, and you are going to walk, sing, and dance. People are waiting for your story; captives are waiting for your story to be told so that they can be set free. You are going to speak it out. It must come out. It must come out. It must come out ..."

Though I had heard God calling me to write my story for over a year, I had been halted by a paralyzing fear and was desperately waiting for solid, beyond all doubt confirmation ...

... and so it begins.

Prologue – The Breaking Point

I grabbed my son and shoved him into his car seat way too hard. Then, putting my face in my little girl's face, I yelled ... harshly, loudly ... it terrified my soul, so what was it doing to theirs? The rage that had been poured into me all those years now seeped out through my own hands. It was then that something inside of me broke. I shattered. I knew I had to find the courage and strength to leave before it was too late; too late for me and too late for those little ones looking up at me. Though at the moment my resolve was set, I had no idea how it was going to happen. I was unraveling quickly. I barely had enough left of anything in me each day to breathe, let alone escape.

Dear Reader,

As you look out at the seemingly endless road ahead of you, you may feel totally overwhelmed. You may be broken, battle weary, and worn, and just not sure how you are going to keep walking, let alone arrive at your destination of wholeness. However, you do not have to get there today. Today you only have to take one step. You can take one step. God showed me a different way of looking at my healing journey; one that has encouraged me along the way.

When I first moved into my home, the yard was overtaken by too many trees--beautiful, but not functional. Branches and trees commanded the space, overtaking the trampoline and suffocating the swing set. A huge evergreen blocked the light and impeded the view from my window. Its needles filled the eavestrough, and the branches scraped against the house. That evergreen made my trek to the water tap a hazardous adventure of ducking under branches, sweeping spider webs out of my face, and avoiding prickly thistles and pine needles.

Thinking about how I could transform that corner of the yard was overwhelming when I looked at it in its entirety, but God gave me a step by step vision for the space. I knew I wanted a patio with a garden strip by the deck, but that is all I knew. I could not see anything beyond that. So, block by block, I laid it down. Once that was completed, I could imagine another little garden with a vine climbing the fence onto the other side. A bed of river rocks with a fountain would eventually join the two gardens. Then came the brick flower bed. It took two summers, but step by step, rock by rock (and one car accident with a full load of those rocks), the overwhelming project was now a beautiful, functional, healing garden. I would spend many hours sitting there during the evenings, listening to the trickling water from the fountain, and watching the reflection of the light dance and play on the side of the house.

In the same way, God can take the messy areas of our lives and transform them, step by step, pruning and chipping away in one section at a time. He reforms it, redefines it, and recreates it until He has your heart, your mind, and your soul just as He wants them. What was once an overwhelming, seemingly insurmountable obstacle (or mess) in our lives can become radically changed, as we allow the Master Builder to take hold of every part of our hearts and surrender our wills, minds, emotions, pride, motives, desires, and everything else, to Him.

In the same way, we may not see the finished project right from the start (being healthy and whole), but we do not have to. He has the plan. We do not have to make it, or even follow it. We just have to follow Him, the author and finisher of our faith, and He will make us healthy and whole. He will make us into who we need to be in order to accomplish all of His purposes for our lives. In reality, it is the simplest of truths yet somehow, also the most difficult . . . . . .

This is my prayer for you, dear Reader!

Create in me a clean heart, O God.

Renew a loyal spirit within me.

Psalm 51:10

For we are God's masterpiece. He has created us anew in Christ Jesus, so we can do the good things He planned for us long ago.

Ephesians 2:10

My child, listen to what I say, and treasure my commands. Tune your ears to wisdom, and concentrate on understanding. Cry out for insight, and ask for understanding. Search for them as you would silver; seek them like hidden treasures. Then you will understand what it means to fear the LORD, and you will gain knowledge of God. For the LORD grants wisdom! From his mouth come knowledge and understanding. He grants a treasure of common sense to the honest. He is a shield to those who walk with integrity. He guards the paths of the just and protects those who are faithful to him. Then you will understand what is right, just, and fair, and you will find the right way to go. For wisdom will enter your heart, and knowledge will fill you with joy. Wise choices will watch over you. Understanding will keep you safe.

Proverbs 2:1-11

Part 1

My Life in Black & White

Just Bruises

One of my many counselors had a practice of reading back to me all she had summarized in our previous session. After our first session, she started reading: "Calli was severely abused …" I stopped her immediately and had her officially change the word 'Severely,' to 'Moderately.' Minimizing and denial were very much still rooted in my heart at the time. Even still, to this day I am quick to clarify that I was never 'Beaten Up,' just 'Roughed Up.' No broken bones and no blood. Just bruises, a displaced rib or two, and great amounts of fear, intimidation and humiliation. Having hands around my throat by someone in a white hot rage, encouraging me to say, "Just one more word," so he would have an excuse to "Crush my larynx" was enough to plant cold terror deep in my heart, easy to be recalled at every instance of trauma. Always just enough physical violence, with the threat of more, to keep me unsure of how far it could go--would go--intentionally or otherwise. Being thrown into a wall just a little too close to the stairs helped to "Keep me in line!"

The expression of "Walking on Eggshells" really does not cut it in circumstances such as these. It is more like walking around with a gigantic anvil continually suspended over your head. Even when times were good and things were on the upswing, deep down in your heart you knew the anvil was there and would eventually crash down on your head, crushing all of you: your heart, your mind, your will, your life, your beliefs, your hopes, your dreams ... every part of you.

This too was a paradox. When it was going well, you truly believed it was over; there would be no more ... it would be okay now. You cling to that tiny spark of hope that *this* time, it would be different ... *this* time, it would be okay.

... But it never was.

My prayers eventually transformed into desperation. I sincerely began to hope that something really bad would happen. Not something bad enough to leave me dead or permanently disabled, but bad enough to give me the okay to be able to leave for good this time.

... I didn't have to wait long.

... My prayers were soon answered.

Establishing a Destructive Pattern

The first time that painfully harsh words were said to me, in my mind the relationship was over. Or so I thought. However, the next time I saw him, it was like nothing had happened. Rob welcomed me with open arms. By the words he had spoken to me, I had thought I was hated, or at least severely disliked, and our relationship certainly had no future. Now here he was, acting like everything was fine. It made me start to question all that had happened. Maybe I was making too big a deal out of it; maybe it wasn't as bad as I thought. He was acting normal about it, so maybe it was more normal than I realized.

I was blessed to have grown up in a household where my parents rarely fought, and from what I heard, harsh words were never exchanged between them. Maybe my parents' relationship was rare. Maybe a few critical remarks here and there were just a part of most relationships. Besides, it wasn't so bad. Little did I know that I was already being conditioned to live in a cycle of abuse.

After this had happened a few times, I talked to a friend about the situation. She asked me if there was more good than bad. At the time, I thought, "Yes, there is clearly more good than bad. He seems to care about me the majority of the time. He is interested in God, and we have so much fun together biking up and down in parkades, going for walks or watching the sunset, wandering around art galleries, enjoying coffee outside on restaurant decks, or listening to music in the dark. It all seemed exciting and peaceful. It seemed right in those moments except for the small interruptions from time to time." I thought, "Yes if that is as bad as it gets, I can handle it!" Maybe I was naïve at the time, but I honestly had no understanding of the destructive patterns that were being established in my life or how much of an under-exaggeration that statement was!

The first time it became physical was ten months into our marriage. It had been established early on that I would attend all his functions, events, and family gatherings. However, after so much sabotaging behavior, (starting a fight at the event then walking out on me, canceling at the last minute, or purposely making us hours late just to name a few), I realized that I was on my own for everything in my world. So, I had been out at a staff function by myself, and when I returned home, he was there with his brother. He made some rude remark to me, and I gave him a smart aleck reply and went on my way, not thinking too much about it. That night, as I crawled into bed, he kicked me hard enough to cause me to fly backward over the nightstand into the wall. We hadn't been fighting, so I, totally uncomprehending his fury, thought he was fooling around. I got up and tried to go back to bed. I don't recall what he said, or I said, if anything, but he began kicking me repeatedly again and said something. This time, I knew he was serious and was intent on hurting me.

Realizing what was happening, I grabbed my keys, ran out, and showed up on my friend's doorstep. I needed a place to stay for the night. This would not be the last time. Many tears fell as I let the reality of what had happened sink in. He had never been physical before. This was a whole new level of abuse. I was absolutely done this time.

When I later showed up on my own doorstep with my parents as protection and support, Rob answered in an attitude of admission and reconciliation. He wanted to work things out. He didn't want to give up on us. I agreed, but somehow, once my parents left, not another word was said. It was all swept under the carpet. I was too scared to bring it up, thinking that we would eventually talk about it when he was ready. Instead, a destructive pattern was firmly established; the only change was that I eventually rarely confessed any physical abuse to my family or my friends. Part of the reasoning for this was to protect them from being worried about me or living in fear for me. Another part was because of the shame I felt for tolerating the abuse. I had my reasons for staying but didn't think they would understand.

Secrecy also made it easier to deny how bad it was getting. As it was, my family became nervous to phone me, thinking they might be getting me at a bad time, and make it worse for me. I only found out much later that if my mom didn't hear from me every couple of days, she feared the worse. Another huge part of starting to hide the abuse is fear. The less that people know, the less chance they have of saying something in front of him that would get me in trouble. Over time, all these patterns became a way of life--destructive and dysfunctional, but still a way of life--my way of life.

A friend of mine wrote a poem and shared it with me (Windows to the Soul). It was about an abused woman, and I was her inspiration. Terribly offended, I wrote back, (Response to Windows to the Soul), lashing out at her and accusing her of being judgmental and not understanding. She wrote back in another poem, apologizing, (Apology in Retrospect), yet standing strong in her opinion. In my final response, many months later, (Apology no. Understanding), I was ready to face the truth a little more directly.

Windows to the Soul

Her eyes speak to me before she makes a sound

They tell her story   hollowly.

They say

I too was once like you

I was a woman,   whole   being

I wept for others   less   whole than me

I wondered why they let others

Compartmentalize their   souls

I fought imaginary battles for them in arenas of hate

too late

I was mortified by their stagnant spirit

stewing in lethargic limbo

I criticized their acceptance of a life

void of

void

I clung to my self-righteous paradigms of

feminist power   illusion   delusion   disillusionment

I broke the chains that bound them to their

beds of thorns   tangled   mangled existences

I imagined assembling the pieces of their broken

beings   fragmented   fermented   forgotten

I made them   whole   again   once more

I too was full   of   me.

Her eyes retreat   hauntingly

Remember me   they echo

Remember me

I will my friend,   my sister   my mother

I will

Response to Windows to the Soul

The worst is the contempt in the eyes
       No. Not him.

          You

Me, as I was

I too, stood strong
       "I would never ..."

          "If it was me ..."

             "I would just leave ..."

But it's not you.

You don't know the depth
       of the hurt ... yes   but the confusion

So easy to say
       I said it too

but when you are in the midst of the storm
       the crashing winds of the words

          wreak havoc on your mind

             and bury your heart

                and stain your soul.

You cannot withstand
       You cannot stand

          You cannot.

But how can I go?
        There is still
            Hope.
"He does not understand -
        These   are the words that will   reach him   touch him."

Now I understand them
        I am them.

Yes, I know you cannot stay
        it will break you
Yes, I know you cannot go
        You cannot go
            while there is still hope.

Apology in Retrospect

She sees my frustration as contempt

I am sorry

I cannot speak these words, though

Defensive

I never meant to hurt her

Never intended to pass judgement on a friend

    Her eyes once again plead with me,

    "Walk a mile in my shoes," they seem to say

    "I'm trying," mine reply

But I don't live in the eye of the storm that is your relationship with him

Have not reaped the sowing disarming disillusionment of wedded bliss

Have not lain with him sated by the consummation of physical love

Have not lived by his smile   snake charmer   charmed   charming

Have not grown accustomed to the countenance of love   fleeting on his face

Have not shared a life with him   sacrifice   compromise
    understanding   hope

Dare I say

Will not

No

For she says that she cannot go while there is a chance that she will reach him   touch him

Hanging onto a thread, I think to myself

A fabric that unravels with every word spoken in anger

    every action that is intimidating

              humiliating

                degrading

                  calculating

                    contemptuous

No. Not me.

Him.

Apology no. Understanding

Yes.

Him.

Unraveling our life together

The angry words tear at the fabric of us   of me.

Built on hopes and dreams and other unrealities

the foundation of us is wavering

      washed away by every tear that is wrenched

         from my soul.

Hope is there.

     Hope is gone.

        Time passes

           The calm before the storm

              Longer this time

              'Maybe never again.'

But there is always an again

'But maybe not this time'

But there are always more tears   more sorrow   more anguish

more.

But do not see me as less than whole

My sister, my friend

Do not make me hide my shame   my fear   my hope

      my care   my heart

If I become afraid to talk to you, it is then I am trapped

      caged   bound

Yes,   my soul hurts

      And my spirit   is bound

            Bound by broken dreams and broken hearts and

      Broken

But do not feel sorry for me.

      There is still some fight left

         I will be ready

My spirit will soar once again

And I will be okay.

Why not Just Leave?

Please take the *just* out of that question when you ask us this. There is no *just* in anything about it. One of the most misunderstood things about living in abuse is why we do not leave. In the beginning, before the anvil shows up, there are still so many good things about the relationship that you do not want to give up on it. I had not failed at anything in my entire life, and my marriage was one of the most important things I had. I did not want to give up on it without exhausting every possible avenue. I felt that if I could work hard enough, love him enough, and say the right things to him, then he would understand what his actions and words were doing to me--how they were tearing out my soul. How could he not understand that? How could he not see the destruction that was happening to not only the relationship but to me as a person?

In between the insanity, he seemed to love me, to care about me, and to protect me, so why would he want to destroy me? Such a small revelation to him could bring a drastic positive change in our lives. The hardest part was that when things were bad, you didn't dare make any comments about anything, let alone challenge him in his behavior. When things were good, you didn't bring up the bad, because, before the anvil sets in, you believe that the bad is over. Things are good now, he gets it, he sees, he understands, so he's not going to let it get ugly again. How could he?

You tell yourself, "Things are amazing now. His card was so sweet, so touching. It is loving now, so fun!" Then, once the anvil appears, you don't dare bring up the bad because that discussion alone will bring with it the bad, and things will get very nasty, very fast.

Another often misunderstood thing about living in abuse, making it not so easy to 'just leave,' is the gradual nature of its escalation. It starts with such small things: a critical word here and there, a small comment that sets in mistrust of family and friends, an argument followed by incredibly loving words on a card, accompanied by flowers. If he were to call you a B**** and grab your face within the first few times you went out with him, you would be quick to leave, but the process is gradual. By the time these small interruptions become huge destructive forces, you are too invested and too entangled in the web to see rationally. As well, because you have dealt with these encounters so regularly, at such a gradually increasing pace, they have become somewhat normalized--in a twisted way--in your world.

Living in it, I didn't see or understand the escalation process until, in a moment of honesty after a counseling session, my abuser explained it to me. He said it was like a drug addiction. He needed more of it; a meaner, more devastating choice of words, a little more physical violence, a new level of humiliation delivered, to get the same "fix." Hence the need for calculated escalation. They are thriving on it while you are barely surviving in it. They don't want to stop the relationship; they are getting what they need from it. It is you who is being dismantled and destroyed. That is why they cannot give it up. They seem to throw you away. Then they do everything they can to get you back, over, and over, again. It is somehow twisted around (abusers are master manipulators) so you end up feeling guilty if you are the one wanting to exit the relationship: "How could you do this to the family? How can you give up on us? I am willing to make the sacrifices necessary to make it work, so how come you too, cannot make the needed sacrifices to save the family for the children?" Black is white, and white is black in the world of abuse.

Another factor for remaining in an unhealthy marriage is economics. Single parenting can drop your standard of living. I was incredibly blessed to have my education and some finances from the sale of our house. Even with this, though, it is difficult. It is hard to make it on our own. For some, it is enough to drive them back. "Where will I go? What will I do?"

Furthermore, single parenting in itself is tough, let alone with someone who can make everything so very difficult. Forcing the kids to live between two houses, (the logistics alone are daunting), the false guilt of breaking up the family "just because your feelings got hurt once in a while," and the realization of having to deal with all the court issues and court costs are all factors. Just the thought of having to walk through all you would have to walk through if you leave, when you can barely hold yourself together on a good day, can be overwhelming enough to prevent you from even making a plan, let alone following through with it.

Realistically, there are as many reasons why women stay in abusive relationships as there are women and relationships, with many variations on the themes. Many involve the FEAR, in which you have been well trained. Of course, there is the "Knight in shining armor" aspect. Again, there is so much irony in the world of abuse, where up is down, and down is up. When things are going well in our world, they go "SO WELL!" It builds up the hope of "this is how it could be!

If only I could ... when he gets it, it is going to be so amazing!" It is SO hard to understand how the very same man who could systematically be destroying every part of me, could be the same man who, so many times, would swoop in and save the day!

When things were going wrong (in some area of my life that he did not initiate), he was the first to champion my cause. He would stand up for me, fight for me, go out of his way to get me what I need, and do everything in his power to right the situation.

When I was in the hospital after surgery, he was the most attentive, caring man I knew, meeting my every need. In my times of stress, he was there by my side, walking me through it. This was the man I knew and loved. This was my knight in shining armor, my prince charming, the one in whom I didn't want to give up. It truly was like living with two different people. You never knew who you were going to get at any moment: the knight who would throw on his boots and gallantly shovel you out as you ungracefully got stuck in the driveway, or the one who would calmly ask, "What the f*** did you do now?" The one who treasured you and made you feel like you were the most special girl in all the world, who you adored and wanted to spend the rest of your life with ... or the one you feared; the one who shoved his fist down your throat just to pull out your heart.

So, you see, it is not easy to 'just leave.' Instead of asking why we do not leave, ask instead, why we stay. That way we do not have to get defensive. When we give our heart and soul, and sometimes our life, to try and honor our vows before God, cherish our family, fight for our belief that perhaps with a bit more work, a little more understanding, a little more help, and we can prevent our family from exploding--we should not have to defend that. If you have been there, you understand. It is so hard to take that final step, to give up hope and realize, yes, all is lost. Sometimes I feel people give up too easily. Sometimes, I know now, we stay too long, and only by losing all, can we regain everything. Things can not--will not--change, without drastic measures. Leaving is the first drastic step. Staying away is the second; sometimes temporarily, often permanently. It is a hard thing, but sometimes it is just not safe to remain in the relationship.

Physical abuse aside, the verbal and emotional abuse alone is enough. It wrecks you. It kills you, one way or another. You are no longer you. You eventually disappear, without even realizing it.

[Journal entry, ten months after I left the marriage]

<u>January 4th, 2009</u>

The feelings came back this weekend. The not being able to breathe, like you just can't get a full breath, shortened, almost gasping. Every once in a while you try to take a deep breath, just to get enough oxygen. Just so constricted. There is a dizziness, lightheaded, like you just can't get connected, can't get grounded. No energy. No feeling, no sparkle, no joy. It's like trying to survive, to put one foot ahead of the other, and do what you have to do, but that is it, no more, no less. You feel like having an all-out cry session, that deep, deep retching crying that comes from your very soul. Maybe that would provide some relief. But you can't. There is no relief. Just this zombie survival state. No energy, no joy, no happiness, nothing, just the numbness that overtakes you, your life, your spirit, soul, your very being.

There is a heaviness, the proverbial load on your shoulders weighing you down. You feel battle worn, like you have fought a war, battle weary, like you have spent all the physical and emotional energy you possess. Like you have had that all out on the floor cry, which you can't have, because there is no release, no relief. There is nothing left, nothing, no room for dreams, for living, for hopes, even fear, just nothing but heaviness. No joy, no dreams, no inspiration, no life. Just the blackness. That state of numbness, of shell shock, of disbelief, of no hope. It just grips you, and won't let go. Your stomach is tense, doesn't want food; tight, tense, like you got kicked in the stomach, or hit by a truck.

It is so hard to live in this state, let alone plan or put a plan into action to get out, to change the circumstances that put you in this state. You can't see past the numbness, can't believe in a bright future. Just surviving. You need to think to breathe ... to breathe without thinking ... that is freedom. (See appendix 3)

Walking Through the Pain

I will let her tell the story of her pain, as she is the one walking through it. Though she is me, I am no longer her, so she will say it best, straight from her heart, as it is happening. I feel bad for what she had to go through. Yet I am thankful to her that she chose to keep walking, as much as it hurt, so she could become all God wanted her to be ... and then find her place on the sideline to cheer on the others.

March 18, 2001

I feel my heart has been broken. This is my journey, set out on to help me understand why and how, and with the risk of sounding melodramatic, to help me become whole.

I keep reading over my journal, and the same words pop up. "I can't keep living like this." Yet I do. The days, weeks, months go by, and I am in the same place, going around in circles, yet sinking lower and lower each time. Am I killing my spirit, my soul? Something has to change. Today it must start! I alternate between having hope for our relationship, and hoping he'll really be physically abusive so I can leave guilt free. Sometimes having hope scares me, as it means possibly the never ending cycle will only continue in a different dance.

It is all about power and control. He has admitted that. He needs to control me. It's like another reality. Words can be said or heard, then denied, whatever works best at the time. It's like a puzzle he does with our lives. He puts the pieces together, each one individual, connected to the rest, but with its own rules and reality. He decides and defines the circumstances and the reality he wants.

[This journal entry is my response to a section in Patricia Evan's book, *Verbal Abuse Survivors Speak Out*.]

This "Story of Disintegration" seems so familiar. I will not quit talking though. But I do talk less. Sometimes I regret ever saying anything, but yet I know I would not be as strong if I hadn't. Sometimes I feel so unfaithful for discussing the situation, and sometimes I think maybe I do talk about it for attention. I have always needed heart to hearts with my friends. Yet I know I did not cause this, nor do I deserve it. This resonates so strongly with me, I had trouble writing it without tears. Ow, it hurts so bad, so deep within. I cry out "Why can't he just like me? Find something about me acceptable?"

That's what I feel like. 'Diminishing' sounds so insignificant, yet I really feel it is destroying me. I still feel successful in some areas, but I really don't know the effect it is having on me. I think I'm still doing O.K. Am I? 'Thingifying,' [a term used in Evan's book that describes how abusers turn people into things in their minds] maybe that's what he's trying to do with his constant criticism. Maybe that's why he rarely phones, to let me know his plans, or phones at the last minute. This ties in with him not allowing me my opinion, belittling or name calling if my opinion differs from his.

He often does this, telling me why I did something. Usually he is so far off, I would never even have rationally imagined it. Then he doesn't believe me when I said his idea is wrong. He really believes he is always right, even about my thoughts/motivations.

March 28, 2001

He continually used to say "because of what you did, (I caused him to be mean.) What the ... did you do?" when I got stuck in the driveway. And then I feel guilty, sort of believing it was my fault.

[This next journal entry is in response to information in Evan's book about how people control others by assigning status.]

He has done this with my teaching, my business and my university. At this point, I don't doubt my competency. He said I would be a terrible mom, but I know I would be awesome.

[This entry is in response to information in the book about the inside environment and the outside environment in an abusive relationship do not correspond, which can be detrimental.]

I think I can. Am I not? Am I changing? How will I know? I think I'm fine. I think I'm strong.

[This is in response to information about the false belief that extreme caring to the abuser would change the behavior toward the survivor.]

This is exactly where I am at. But since we've been on a 'good run' for 1 and 1/2 weeks, it's easy to keep thinking this. I am curious and anxious to how and when the next blow up will occur, and how I will deal with it. Will I still (or again) decide to leave? Am I naïve enough to believe that since I told him I'd leave if it keeps happening, that he'll change? Why haven't I talked to anyone? Am I scared of being accountable?

August 31, 2001

Said he had enough. We were done. I defied him. I don't have the same vision. Said I had to get out of the bedroom. We'd separate.

September 4, 2001

He didn't call T [his secretary] until 2:00 p.m. He said he's not going to put himself through this for nothing. I don't deserve anything, and he can work as an electrician for 6 months, and go on unemployment. He called me a b**** and a c***. First time he called me that. He said it twice, and that I blew it. He wants to hold me responsible for him quitting his career. He says why should he do it if he can't do it for someone. I need to make this my last straw. I said he needs to call the real estate agent by Friday or I will. He said females are all stupid and can't do anything right. He really has no respect for women.

September 11, 2001

Said he wants me to leave, so he'll buy me out for $20,000. The next day, when I asked him if the bank would let him carry the mortgage alone, he flipped the story, saying if I left I'd leave him in financial ruin, I'd wreck his reputation, and he'd go bankrupt, and lose his business license. When I said what did he care if he lost his license, he was quitting? He said, " Are you stupid? I'm not quitting." I reminded him that was what he said the other day. He said maybe he felt like it at the time.

Ended argument by saying he didn't want to be with me.

[This poem was the outpouring of my heart as I finally gave up hope and came to terms with the fact that our marriage was over.]

It is time

There is no hope.
The proverbial last straw
Came and went and came
And reared its ugly head
Once more and again
And again
And finally it has won.
It has taken my breath
With the shock and disbelief
Of my world as it whirls
And swirls and dips out of
Control and out of reality and
Out
Out of my mind
And my heart flow the tears and
The pain but the shock has
Left me numb; numb to not feel
And blind to not see and
Broken to not heal.
What do " I " want my friend asks me.

But I'm scared to find the "I"
For fear the selfishness he says I am
Will show its face and be
Real and I'll be the horrible person
He has tried to make me believe
I am yet how can I be so
When it takes everything inside
Of me to just hold it all together
And make it through another day
And laugh and smile and
Wear my mask that helps me
Keep it all together for fear
Of revealing would reveal all and
All would pour out with
Nothing to hold me together and
There would be nothing left but the
Shell of despair and nothing.
But what do I want.
I want to live, to be loved, to
Not be scared to feel to believe to hope.
To be acknowledged,
have someone be proud of me,
Be nice to me, to like me for me and
All the normal things that have become
Dreams for me in my fragile world of illusion.
I want to be greeted with a

Smile in place of the hate that
Cuts deep into my soul trying to
Bleed me into
Believing that it is not good enough
I am not good enough I deserve
Nothing I am Nothing.
I want to smash the mask that
Hides the pain and
Stop the lies that are my
Life and be able to say
"I'm really OK"
Without the flashes of fear and
Fights of the night rewinding
Through my mind like a plague as I
Smile and say "I'm fine" I'm always fine
I say yet what I want is to be
Free to be me, to love, care, feel, dream,
To stop the tears that flow for weeks and
Leave me with a mind that cannot think,
A heart that cannot feel and a
Spirit where the light cannot shine
And that's the life that has become mine.
But. There is no hope. So I am free.

Why am I the one who feels guilty when I am the one who has been hurt almost beyond what I can bear? It has become a physical disintegration along with the psychological, as I hurt not only in my spirit and mind, but my body is reacting too. My head hurts and my stomach aches. I wonder when I'll have my 'sparkle' back. Once again I say to myself," I can't keep living like this." But this time it's different. He has gone too far in what he said, and his attempts to manipulate. I feel if I don't leave this time, I never will be able to. Yet my friend says no, don't say that, it may take 'leaving in stages,' 2 or 3 times to go through with it, so don't beat yourself up if you don't. My 'circle of support' is widening. I've added 4 more people. I've learned that I will not be able to walk away freely and easily, like I thought I would when I hit my last straw. But she said" no, it will be hard, and your heart will be broken, as you have invested a lot and you are losing a lot. But you need to leave to preserve yourself. God doesn't want you in a relationship that is destroying you. And it is destroying you. The only times you are happy is when you are away from him, or the odd time when he is nice to you. You are not in a marriage, you are in the destruction of a marriage."

I need to get my ducks in a row. I need to break the recorder in my head. I need to block the guilt, the false guilt, that I am doing something wrong by leaving. It has been his choice. His words and actions for years have been telling me he doesn't want me. And you know what? He doesn't deserve me. I am a bit scared. What will he do when I leave?

September 18, 2001

Tried talking. He said I betrayed him when I defied him. He can't trust me because I don't think like him. We need one vision (but his way, his plan). I said, how can I trust him when he lies, like about quitting work. He then denied that incident took place! [He said] Now he knows I'm crazy because it didn't happen - me saying it just proves I'm crazy.

In October of 2001, I made a plan to leave. I found a place to go. I sorted as much of my belongings as possible, without being obvious. On a Saturday, when he was at work, I called in the people I had prearranged to come. They helped me pack and load up all the things that were mine before we were married. Anything I brought into the house, I took with me. Anything that he had brought in, I left. Anything that we bought together, including the appliances, I left. We had been married for three years, three months. We did not have any children.

October 5, 2001 – (night before I left)

Had to keep talking to people tonight to go through with it. Good thing I had a conference to keep me busy all day. Dad had strange dream, woke and prayed, and had 'vision' Rob would do anything to win me back, then do whatever it took to make sure I didn't leave him again. He would do this by killing me in a way that was 'accidental' like slow poisoning or cut brake line. Overactive overprotective father or warning, as I sit here with a cold sore 'predicted' or seen by Mom.

October 6, 2001

D. Day. Lots of people to help. Talked to C and B on the phone in the a.m. It kept me sane. I felt like I was dying. I kept going into hyperventilation, and had trouble stopping. This never happened to me before. 3 or 4 times, I would do this, until phone rang or sat down – got dizzy. The people were excellent. Very supportive. L says they all decided if I was to go back, I'm on my own, nobody will help me. I laughed. I knew what they meant.

It was so hard. I am so worried about his reaction. How would I feel coming home to an empty house? He is so busy and stressed with work. I have to remember he kicked me out initially.

I would not have chosen this time. I probably would not have left. Will he be scared, lonely, sad, or just angry? Will he try to get in touch with me, or just write me out of his life? I'm scared, a little, and jump at noises. But part of me thinks he'll try to erase me from his life as quickly as possible. Why couldn't he admit he is abusive and get help? I have to remember my pain, and what he put me through, so I can stay strong. I feel so sad, it hurts. I keep second guessing myself, but I had "that conversation" too many times. S said I was like a flower. I was being stepped on, not watered or fed, but still expected to bloom & thrive. He did that to me, yet expected me to stay, be loving and respectful, and do everything he told me to, have my own opinion, yet it could not be different from his. Nothing was ever good enough for him. Yet I still think of him as a sad, lonely little boy. Will he be sad, or did he really not love me, and just be angry that I "caused him to lose the house." How can he expect me to stay when he always was so mean to me? I know he didn't beat me, the physical violence was very minor, 5 or 10 incidents of low level, without bodily harm, but he had said "I only don't beat you because I don't want to." What happens when he wants to? Is he capable of murder? He told me "everyone is capable of murder if the circumstances are there." I guess

I don't really want to find out. S said the physical violence usually starts during pregnancy.

I have so many feelings, I am trying to allow myself to feel, yet only a little at a time, otherwise it would be way too overwhelming. One foot in front of the other. One step at a time.

November 21, 2001

He didn't do anything when I left. Part of me thanks God for that, and part of me cries. It will be 7 weeks on Saturday. The heavy, oppressiveness that was continually weighing me down, crushing me, sapping the life out of me, is gone. My friends say "Welcome back." I have life in my eyes again. And I do. I feel alive, but I am still sad, and still wondering. I am no longer ashamed to make eye contact with people. I no longer have anything to hide. I can be me. And I like me. I do, however, have to figure out what is me, and how much I have lost. I know a lot was preserved, but I'm unsure of how much has changed because of my experience. I feel stronger now, and perhaps even wiser. I do feel like a survivor. And I know that I cannot, will not go back to that life. He supposedly is in counseling, or has agreed to go, as a prerequisite to reconciliation. But even that scares me, as how do I know what is real, and what is "reeling me in?" Most of me thinks it's his game to keep stringing me along to keep my name on the mortgage, to keep what he considers his property. But part of me wants to really believe he is sorry and realizes how much he has lost when he lost me. Part of me is so glad he hasn't contacted me, yet part of me wishes he had at least tried. I have nightmares that we'll be together again, then he'll do something to me. Is that intuition, fear or over dramatization, since I've read so much on what can happen? I feel like I need to start dealing with things, as I have been avoiding it. But S [one of the professors from the university, who began to counsel me] says that's O.K. I will when I am ready. I'm tired of being the sad, scared little girl. I want to love life, laugh & love. I want to feel free. I don't want to hurt anymore.

I remember, in the first little while after I moved out, I wanted to take a razor to my arms. Not in a suicidal way, but just as a way, one slash across the arm and I'd split open like a balloon and all the hurt and pain would come out. Since I told S about it, I haven't felt that need. She says maybe, since I think so much in metaphor, that it was symbolic for the release of pain I felt I needed. I think that is true. I hope so, because it sounds so psycho.

I'm in a pretty good headspace. I'm seeing friends, and being pretty open with people. I'm not a pile on the floor, like I thought I might be. I am going to church, and trying to get to know people there. I'm O.K. I will be O.K. Time to start journaling every day, and reading Rebuilding. I need to be rebuilt; to work on me.

Friday, November 23, 2001

The hardest time is at night. As I face the evening alone, I put off going to bed. It is so sad. I cry. I never got married to cry alone at night. How could he have been so mean to me? Why did he do this to me? I miss him, yet I hate him. I hurt so much. Did he ever love me, or was it always a game? Will it always be a game?

The movies are not like this. Boy meets girl, boy gets girl, boy threatens and hurts girl, and looks at her with contempt when he makes her cry. Well Rob, I am crying. Do you feel better now? Why did you hurt me so? God, what is the plan for my life? Are you going to 'fix' Rob? I know he has to want to change; everyone has free will. What lessons do you want me to learn in all this? Will it

end? Will I be happy? Or will I forever be alone?
Is that my destiny? Always and forever alone?

Wednesday, November 28, 2001

Sometimes I say something and the tears are so
close to the surface, it shocks me. I don't have a
journal with me at the time, usually, and I don't
always remember what I said or thought about.
One thing I do remember, today, talking to S, is
that I don't want to be where I am at - alone,
starting over. As well, I'm really scared he'll want
me back for my finances only. Selling the house
will be the only way I'll even start to trust him.
Maybe not even then. Can you say ' manipulation?' I
can't go back to that life. Yet I don't want to be
alone all my life. I feel so trapped, helpless, out of
control. G talked to him today. Our prayer is that
he can recognize any hints of manipulation. I fear
I'll cave, but S told me a story about one man who
left, and did so in order that his wife would beg
him to come back, and then he would go back, but
this time with the ultimate in power and control.
He would be king of the castle. But it did not turn
out that way. His plan did not work. She did not
beg him to come back. If she did, he would know
how much control he had. She would have to agree
to anything. He could do what he wanted, with the

threat of leaving. If I go back, he would have the power, and I" would always go back, they always do..." so he thinks. I cannot allow myself to do that.

December 29, 2001

The hardest part is at night. It's not right to be alone, night after night, all my life. I don't understand why this is. I know it could be worse, but that doesn't make me feel any better. Rob has talked to Mom and Dad twice. He apologized, in tears, for how he has treated me. Is it real, or is it a ploy? He would have to prove to me it's not the finances he wants back. I have learned from experience that he will do or say anything if he thinks that will get him what he wants. He is supposed to be talking to the pastor from my sister in law's church. G asked if he could talk to him about what he knows. I said the pastor could call me. I really want to talk to him. I want to meet with Rob, and see if I can tell where he is at. I feel like other people would be disappointed if I 'gave in.' But how do I know if there has been a heart change? We pray for a miracle; maybe there will be one. Maybe we are supposed to believe for one. I'll call the pastor Monday if I haven't heard from him.

Nights have been really hard. I'm scared to go to bed and not sleep right away. This morning I figured out why. I don't want that stop and think time. I've been avoiding any prayer time, thinking time, deep reading time, or doing anything alone that would put me in touch with my thoughts. I've watched 8 movies or more in 2 days. As soon as I stop, I think and feel, and that is tormenting me. I feel like ripping my heart out. I feel like doing something crazy so they'll 'take me away' for a while. I just want to turn everything off for a while.

But you can't always choose the situation, but you can choose what you'll do with it (Lord of the Rings!) I should be able to take my power back, and be empowered enough to be able to 'stop' it myself, without having to have my control taken away. I feel like I'm maxed out without anything else, and I don't feel like I can handle anything. I don't know how I'm going to get through Jan & Feb, especially, then comes SPLASH [a big musical/theatrical event I was directing at my school] and Italy [I was to chaperone a high school trip]. I won't be done until April. Then, when am I going to do my project? [I was working on my project for my Master's degree. I only had 5 years to complete it once I started, and I was coming up on the deadline.]

I just can't seem to wrap my head around anything, big or little.

God, my prayer is that you'll help me get through this, day by day, with Your strength, dignity and grace. Reveal to me Rob's real heart, away from the games, lies & manipulation. Show me who speaks the truth. Help me not waste my holiday with activities that just shut me down & make me avoid life. Help me eat better and exercise. Help me take care of myself. Help me slow down, and take stock of my heart. Help me listen to myself. Help me know the truth. Help me stop my destructive behavior and thoughts. Amen

Sometimes I think I am going slightly psychotic, but I know it is just my expression of pain. This is my journey. I don't know why I am in this place. But God, help me to learn what I must learn while I am here. I have so much emotion in my heart. I want so much to do something with my life. I want to affect people somehow. I don't want to go through life in a little cocoon. I want to stop pouting, and enjoy life. I want to be into something that can express me fully. I want to stop putting my life on hold until ' I get out of this place I'm in,' but live now, live fully. Life is the journey. Not the end. If I want to be done, like I claim, that would mean I would like to be done my life. I don't want that. I'm not ready for that, even though sometimes I think about it too much. I would like to be done stuff I always seem to have to do and get on with things I want to do instead of have to do. I do find I am too busy. I need to reevaluate my priorities. I need to discover what is important to me. I always feel' once I get done this ...' Yes, I do need to get done some stuff, and that will take some pressure off, i.e. the bulletin,

[I was in charge of doing the quarterly news bulletin for an education committee],   but mostly my project. That will take a big stress off, but I can't seem to get my head around it. It seems too much. But, that was how the bulletin started, but it is beginning to be under control. I need to mobilize my inner resources, even though they seem to be mobilized to just survive and get through. This is where you come in Lord. I need you.

Help me with my stuff, Rob, my relationships & my thoughts. I'm tired of being' on the edge.' I'm tired of depressing, avoiding, and being in survival mode. I'm tired of living my life at arm's length. I'm tired of being scared to stop because maybe I'll think. I'm tired of not being able to turn my head off of the pressure of things long enough to enjoy the non-pressure activities. I'm tired of feeling like I have to have everything else done before I can stop and enjoy any other activities. I think that is why I can't do art. I feel how can I take the time to do that when I have so much other stuff to do? But then life passes you by ...

And going back would not be any different. Living like that, was what got me here. Going back now would put me right back. I have to remember I feel pain now, but not that constant, continued, fall on the floor in anguish kind of pain that I had almost once a week. I don't have to be on guard all the time. It's hard where I am. But I have to remember, I would not exist much longer as me, if I stayed. I never thought I'd be where I'm at, but I have to remain strong. I have to know if there is a heart change in Rob; an attitude & belief system change. I am no longer scared, he's handled it well, but I have to know it is real. This will take time. I cannot leave this place for 6 months. But we will have to meet soon. I've been avoiding that too. Decisions have to be made. What do I do?

<u>January 3, (2:30 a.m.)</u>

I went to the house today. I needed to see if he was O.K. He had a couch, and some books and papers that indicate he is working on himself. If people have been praying for him, why shouldn't we believe the Lord can change him? Other people worry when I even mention him changing. They don't want me to go back. I don't want to go back, not without a lot of change. I can't go back to living like that. I am finally living without the huge oppression I have been feeling. I still crash & cry a lot. But I built myself a healing garden, complete with trees, vines, Greek statues, lights and a couple of angels. I know I need to heal. I know I have been stripped of a lot of what was me. Painting my statues felt good. I know I need to keep doing things for me. And doing the bulletin (once I got over wanting to throw my dad's computer through the window), I am kind of getting excited about doing it. The draft copy turned out pretty well. And I have some ideas for the next one, so maybe I can do this. It's funny; I had such trouble getting a handle on it. Just like my project. But once I got started & into it, it was O.K. I can do it. I just hate new stuff, and don't feel 'up to any new challenges.' I hope my project is like that: not bad once I start. Lord help me. It's really stressing me.

Anyway, back to the house. He didn't throw anything out [any of my stuff that I did not take--although later I found out he did rip up our wedding picture], just put it all downstairs. He wiped all traces of me out of the upstairs. It's all in one small corner in the basement. It's funny how easily one can be erased.

He did say he would make me insignificant. So, about reconciliation ... does he want it? Does he really love me, or want to use me, or just not to 'lose?' I have to check the credit line activity. It is higher by 1-2 grand than I think it should be.

Going to the house, I was shaking a little, but being there felt almost normal. But I'm feeling more at home here now. Having V & G home makes its easier. I really missed them. [I was living in the basement suite of a friend's house, and they had been away.]

I do feel a sense of closure. I know he's O.K. I know we need to settle, so I'll probably see him soon. I think I've started to let go.

January 26, 2002

I feel good. I'm very busy, like always in January, but I've almost made it through my second busiest month. February is my busiest. I bought a camera, two more angels to paint, and have made it through my tournament [I coached the junior girls basketball team at my school] (B side winners), finished the bulletin (it's in the mail), am going to Italy in April, and have decided to plan to go to Belize next Christmas. Life is good. Step by step, I'll get through, and enjoy it along the way!

Now ... I met with the pastor for 4 hours, and gave him my version of our 'story.' I asked if he wanted the edited or unedited version, then let it fly. Not everything, never everything, but a lot, very blunt. He has been working with Rob. He is supposedly a Christian now. He goes to church and wants to go on with God, whether or not he can have his marriage restored. Maybe it's true. He has had lots of people praying for him. I'm skeptical though. He has to prove it to a lot of people. Time will tell. I'm meeting with him and the pastor Tues. Against the advice of my 'counselors' I'm not taking anyone with me. I don't think I'll be fooled. I do believe I'm strong, and I'll recognize manipulation. At this point, it is easier for me to keep walking away than to go back and start over, so it is no longer a question of giving in and going back like it would have been before. Meeting with the pastor was emotionally exhausting, but it didn't throw me. The pastor made Rob watch Sleeping with the Enemy. I suggested the video It's not Like I Hit Her. He watched it, said it was hard, and maybe watched it again. He indicated (through the pastor) that it was hard to watch, and he saw himself in it. Maybe there is hope for change. I acknowledge this mentally, not emotionally. He is the type that can change if he wants to. God can help him, but he has to want it. One main issue is the house/credit line. He has put way too much money on it, indicating he is paying my half of the mortgage with the credit line. What is legally appropriate? Can I still be liable/morally responsible for 2 accommodations? I know I am liable for our mortgage, but what about the credit line? Can my lawyer get me off that? It makes me suspect he is still wanting reconciliation primarily for the money. I will question him on that. He told the pastor he will do whatever I ask in regards to the house, yet will he try to manipulate me into staying there, and paying my ½ so he doesn't lose face, or lose the house? I love our house, but I will always be suspicious as to whether he reconciled only for it, and settling for me. I could never be sure. How can we keep the house with the underlying suspicion?

The pastor says he only counsels the more challenging cases. Yah, that's us. Not quite the title I would have liked in my life, but it's been quite a ride. It's taught me lots, and added a new depth to me. Crisis always does.

That was the last entry in the journal. Four months later, I went back into the relationship. We did not sell the house. I truly was convinced he had changed. We used to joke together about "What happened to the old Rob? He's tied up in the basement!" and we'd laugh.

Four months after that, the abuse started again. It escalated quickly. He had fooled everyone. Perhaps he had made real progress, but the voices in his head eventually got the best of him. Our seven-month separation eventually became known as "the little stunt I pulled."

This time, there was a great deal more at stake. I was now three months pregnant.

The Breaking Point

I remember grabbing my son and shoving him into his car seat way too hard, then putting my face in my little girl's face, and yelling ... harshly, loudly. It was terrifying to my soul, so what was it doing to theirs? The rage that had been poured into me all those years was now seeping out of my hands. It was then that something inside of me broke. I knew I had to find the courage and strength to leave ... before it was too late. Though at that moment my resolve was set, I had no idea how it was going to happen. I was unraveling quickly. I had barely enough of anything left in me each day to breathe ... let alone escape.

As I reached that point, the very pinnacle of my tolerance, it was as though I could no longer contain it all. It was too much. It was overflowing. I was overflowing, and I could not--would not--stop it. An insignificant comment by a friend led me to say, "All is not as it seems..." and the dam broke. Soon it all came pouring out of me ... everything ... my whole story ... the secrets, the lies, the abuse, the fear ... all was revealed. Nothing could block the torrential flow once it was released, nor could it be put back into its secret place of hiding.

The mom's group from a neighboring church became a safe sounding board, once I dropped the initial bomb that was my prayer request. After recovering from the stunned silence of the group, the leader and another friend became people I could call to help me sort out things in my muddled, exhausted brain. I told my family doctor what was happening. She offered to help me pack if that would help get me out of there.

Though I had not been totally transparent with my mom, she knew me, and could see I was being dismantled. She encouraged me to get help. I called a woman from the church (now one of my closest friends), and the first thing she had me do was recommit my life to Jesus (see recommitment prayer, in Strategic Survival). We talked through many things, mostly to realign my thinking, as I was basing my beliefs on what my abuser said or did. You cannot think straight if your plumb-line for truth is based on words that were manipulative, deceitful, and controlling. I had to retrain my thought patterns and see things from God's perspective, not from Robs--the one he constantly fed me. She encouraged me to get my "ducks in a row," and be ready in case all hell broke loose ... again. If I did what she suggested--pack an overnight bag with clothing, keys, copies of important papers, medication, journals, etc., and stash it at a friend or family member's home--I would have to admit to myself that things were dire.

As well, at that point I was intent on making it through the spring and summer, and enjoying the parts of it that I could, in my own home, without any more disruption and chaos than was my normal life. Besides, I was determined that I was going to do absolutely everything in my power to rescue my family and get my marriage back on track. Therefore, if in the end I found that I had to leave, I would know in my heart that I had exhausted each and every possible thing that I could say, do, feel, think, believe ... no matter what it took. I regret not taking this wise advice ... for very shortly after this, all hell did break loose.

Around the same time, another friend of mine, a self-proclaimed "neurotic lawyer," became an ally in my plight as my secrets invaded her life. Feigning a headache and giving her theatre ticket to me, she spent the night trying to sort out my situation. She arranged a Pro Bono appointment with the best family lawyer in her firm. "Just," she told me, "to get information." This "information" would come into play quicker than I realized at the time.

[I wrote this poem as I hit my breaking point again. It was twelve days before I left for good...March 5/2008

You don't understand
Why won't you just understand
You can't understand
Just leave you say ...
　　　　Just leave.
But how do I rip the
heart out of my little boy
Out of my four year old.

He won't understand
He can't understand
He just looks at him
With love in his heart

And my heart
            just breaks
to know it can't last
I can't last
            much longer.

It just takes longer and longer
to pick up the pieces
            of me
As I lay shattered
Shattered and broken
            on the ground

With nothing left to FIGHT
And it will be SUCH a FIGHT
He has told me
Oh it will be a FIGHT.

But I have no strength
No strength
            for more
for more than just getting through
            just getting through the day
with a smile on my face

looking into their smiling faces
not knowing that their world
                   is about to shatter
is about to come crashing down around them
So I sacrifice myself.
I sacrifice myself to spare them.
But when will it stop sparing them
When will it stop ...
                   It won't.
But I have no strength to face it ALL

And it will be ALL.
ALL consuming
ALL hatred
ALL anguish
ALL confusion for my little ones.
They will not understand.
I cannot fight them too.

But What DO I DO?
I just want to SCREAM ...
        SCREAM and let it out
        SCREAM and let Me out
        Scream so I can breathe

I   just   want   to   breathe

I know it all
I've read it all
I've thought about it
              a million times
But I am just not released
I'm   trapped.
Trapped of my own making
I know.
Trapped in a façade   a delusion
It's not life   it's not love   its not ...
But I just don't see the way OUT
Can't know the way out
There is no win
There is no hope
There is no happy ending
There is only...There is only.

I   just want   to   breathe
I   just   want   to   breathe ...

        and so I write ....

Đ-Day Number Two

March 19, 2008

Well, I didn't have to wait too long to see the direction my life was taking. He crossed the line, definitely this time, giving me a total release. At 1:15 a.m. on Monday (March 17th) he assaulted me (again), and threatened to kill me. He punched me in the arm every time I looked away from him during our 'discussion.' Then he grabbed me and flipped me over, pinned me down with his body weight, and shook me, grasping my wrists and pulling my upper body right up, then throwing me back down [repeatedly]. He held me right up to his face and said "Do you want to die? Do you ever want to see your kids again?"

[At that question, something inside of me snapped. He had threatened to kill me before, but this time it was different. This time he was directly threatening to destroy my kids' lives by taking their mother from them. It was no longer an attack on me, it was an attack on them. I finally understood that in order to protect them, I had to protect myself. In order to preserve them, I had to preserve myself. It was this connection, this realization that changed everything … I would do everything in my power to save them. And this meant saving myself.]

Then he asked me if I would do everything I could to make this marriage work. I said "No." For some reason he left me alone. I quickly left the bedroom. He followed me asking "What are you doing?" I said "sleeping with [our boy]. He went and woke him up and took him into bed with him. He took our girl into bed with him as well. I couldn't leave without the kids. I didn't know if I should call the police or not. Maybe I should have, [Yes. That was a huge mistake.] but thought that when he was released he would be really furious, better I wait and leave in the morning with the children.

I laid in my boy's bed and barricaded the door. I heard a kitchen drawer being opened and I absolutely froze in terror. What would he need in a drawer? I thought he was getting a knife, to prevent me from leaving, or to follow through on his threat. Shortly after, my daughter came to get me and wanted me to sleep in her bed. I went with her. He came to the door and said if I was thinking about laying charges, he would be fired. I barricaded the door, and lay awake all night. Once a toy horse fell off the bed and fell on a metal tin and I just about hit the roof. I had so much adrenaline in my system there was no way I was going to sleep.

I got up the next morning @ 6 or so and did some work & packed some clothes for the kids. I pretended everything was normal, packed his lunch, made breakfast & had the kids say 'bye' to dad because I had a doctor's (lawyer's) appointment. [This was the appointment my friend had scheduled for me just for informational purposes.] As soon as I was in the car I raced to get them buckled in, panicked & got out of there. I went to a friend's, who was going to babysit my kids anyway. I got the kids settled in, then broke down. I had a bruise on my wrist, a [4 inch] bruise on my shin, 2 small ones on my arm, jaw, sore back, and a rib out of place in my back.

It has been building really badly for this past year.

[The violence, threats, and unrealistic expectations had been increasing. I had no longer been journaling. I was not telling anyone.]

His derogatory remarks were getting worse; he found every opportunity he could to slam me. He had gotten physical with me several times in February/March of last year...

[My friend knows a homicide detective. The detective recommended that I file a police report. I regret that I did not do so. It would have made some of the things I later had to deal with easier. But ... I did not go back. With God's help, I slowly rebuilt my life. And now I am writing this to hopefully help even one person, to stand strong. To let them know that yes, it is hard, so very hard, but not nearly as hard as what you have already endured. Not nearly as hard as what you have already walked through. Have courage. Have faith. Turn your whole heart to God. He really will get you through this.]

April 18, 2009

Today is one of those days. I feel like screaming!!!

AYYYYYYYYYYYYYYYY!

Last night I was depressed and lonely. Everything seems scattered. Floating around disconnected, ungrounded. I have so many half-done jobs around the house, they are very representative of my state of mind. Everything is incomplete, no closure, spinning around out of control ...

"I'll scream later." I have to have an all-out cry session. Something has to break. Something has to break. Something has to change. I need a fall down on your knees healing/God experience. I want to be whole, live my life full & free. I just feel so anxious. I need peace. I want to talk to someone that has been through it but is stable, Christian and way out the other side. I need focus. I need connection. I need I need I need.

Aghhhhhhhhhhhhhhhhhhhhhhhhhhh!!!!

Ahhhhhhhh!

He is laying so much pressure on me. He is still trying to squeeze and push and slam and force me. He says I don't get it. How can I even begin to work on reconciliation, when I left because of his heavy handedness, and he is using the same method to get back together? I can't stand it. I feel like puking. He'll never change. Why can't I get it? Why do I keep hoping? What do I hope for? Who do I talk to? What decisions do I make on what specifically to do? ... I feel stressed, depressed, heavy, spinning out of control. I would be exactly the same as before if we were together. What do I do?

My life feels like a novel. Rob always said reality is more interesting & unreal etc. than fiction. I still don't know what to do, but I know I can't get back in relationship with him. He was brutal to me during the marriage. He was brutal to me in the separation. Now he wants to try " love and forgiveness." This being on the tail end of death threats to anyone coming between him and his family. Death threats? Come on, is this even real? How can this even really be my life? How did it even get to this point? The crazy thing is how he can be so 'normal' the next day, as if none of this even happened? One of the people that felt that they were being threatened is going to lodge a complaint against him. It will be a shock to him. He will be furious. And the crazy thing is even though it is totally consequence for his actions, I feel sorry for the guy. When he is in his 'normal' phase he can be a good guy and loving father. How can he turn so wicked so quickly? I get sucked in when he is in his nice phase. I just so hope his wicked phase is going to go away, to not be real. The pastor said I had to face the truth. Face reality. The reality is he is dangerous when he doesn't get what he wants. There will always be times when he doesn't get what he wants. I would have to sacrifice all of me to the point of dysfunction if I were to be in that relationship. I would have to do what he says, which can be extreme, and say what he wants me to say. I couldn't have an opinion, or friends. The tie with my family would be very strained. He will get violent with the kids whether I am there or not. That is the reality. What good can come out of reconciling? The kids would learn that it is acceptable to treat someone like he treats me.

He hasn't stopped being abusive, so why would he stop it if I went back? It would teach him: "Wow. I treated her like that and she still came back. There is no stopping me now." He has to be stopped. The cycle & chains have to be broken. God, I need your peace, strength and healing.

Picking up the Pieces ... Again

It is all fuzzy and sort of surreal ... two years or so of a haze, sorting out, trying to pick up the pieces that lay shattered on the floor, and reclaim my life. I had to do it this time. The stakes were so much higher now. I had to be strong for my children. I had to break the cycle that had been perpetuated, perhaps for many generations.

I remember going to my friend's house, getting my kids settled, walking halfway across the living room and collapsing. I was wearing a purple shirt ... and I was cold ... so very cold ... I could not stop my teeth from chattering. I remember crying uncontrollably, trying to do it away from my kids, but my three-year-old catching me, pushing my hair out of my face, and trying to comfort me.

I remember being at the lawyer's office, totally numb, making it through in a daze. I remember my friend having to take me places to get things done--paperwork or something--one thing each day ... she would have to walk me through each one.

I remember those first few nights--I hated the nights--all three of us on a pull out bed, awake many hours, my heart jumping and pounding at every creak; wondering when he was going to show up at the door ... what he would do. I remember often waking up in horror, feeling like I just had a nightmare, and then that sweet rush of release as you realize that it was just a dream ... then the plummet of your heart and soul as it dawns on you that no, this is indeed, your reality. I remember the turmoil of my thoughts as my mind frantically tried to come to terms with a situation that was impossible to understand.

I remember stealing away to my home to grab some things, my friend's husband at the door, standing as a sentinel to watch over me, wondering why I was the one repeating "I'm so sorry, I'm so sorry, I'm sorry," as I thought of what this was going to do to my kids.

I remember going to my parents' house for Easter, blinds drawn, kids told not to answer the door … reminiscent of a time in my childhood when we were told to stay away from the windows, as my mom sat at the kitchen table with my auntie, the conversation pausing every time we came into the room.

I remember having to go to the lawyer's office on my birthday. Ironically, it was not one of my worst birthdays ever. I remember going to a job interview, totally broken, only God's grace pulling me through.

I remember God's miracles and timing, as He worked in my life to get us the perfect place to live. Despite the constant sabotage with the sale of our house, everything filed into place, and the house my friend and I claimed in prayer was mine. I would spend the whole summer painting the walls eleven different colors, part of the mindless therapy I needed to get me through.

I remember the neighbor, welcoming me with a plate of cookies. She would soon become a dear friend, brave enough to run interference for me when I needed it, even when he turned on her.

I remember running out of a church service in tears, as the frustration and despair overtook me. Rob's constant attacks would replay in my mind, as he carried out his plan of "not making this easy for me." Receiving prayer from the friend who grabbed me and calmed me down as I ran, was the only thing that kept me from exploding.

I remember meeting other women, whose lives too, had been stolen by domestic violence. My soul was screaming out with the injustice of it all. I remember their horror stories ... the breaking of hearts as mothers forced their sobbing children out their doors and into the waiting cars because they would be the ones arrested if they did not ... of being constantly dragged into court over ridiculous matters, supported by the deep pockets of his parents, depleting every resource she had in the fight ... as if pulling up with a moving truck and taking everything wasn't enough.

I remember seeing their living conditions--things falling apart around them--because they had no one to help them, and no money to fix it. I remember being so thankful for my education and my job, that would ensure that I too would not be destitute and we would not, as Rob had threatened to ensure, "Be living in a box by the side of the road." I remember being so thankful for my almost 80-year-old dad, who would hop up on my rooftop to clean my eaves after the big storm ... then do the same for the old guy next door. I remember being so thankful for my mom, my sister and brothers, my in-laws and my friends, who would help me at every turn ... and I wondered what they do, the others like me, when they have no one. How do they make it ... who helps them?

I remember the night that words and phrases started surfacing in my brain, relentlessly, warding off all sleep until I got up in those late hours and wrote the first underground article for the Christmas Cheer Fund, a campaign to raise money for the fight against domestic violence (See Appendix 1). The seeds for this book already then, were unknowingly planted.

I remember seeing my friend's horrified face as she broke a dish when helping me unpack. I laughed in response, saying, "In my world, a broken dish is really NOT a big deal!" Years later, as I sat sniffling on the floor after smashing almost the entire box of those same dishes ... I burst out into an uncontrollable belly laugh as I realized that I was crying over broken dishes! How far I had come! I remember going camping with that friend, our families joined together for a time, helping me to give my kids experiences that I was not yet ready to give them on my own ... feeling supported, feeling hopeful that life would, indeed, be okay again.

I remember my family and friends still needing to be my backbone when I had none. I remember my friend giving me a bracelet she had made. It became a symbol of power and freedom, reminding me of how she would put her hands on my shoulders with each visit, and say, "You cannot go back." I remember my sister often reminding me that I left because my house was on fire. And that it is still on fire, so I cannot go back.

I remember the 2:00 a.m. phone calls, waking me, my body shaking with fear and adrenaline, until I realized he only wanted to go around the same mountain again, and thought nothing of calling at all hours.

I remember going to church and finally surrendering to the unstoppable, soul cleansing tears that I could no longer contain, and allowing Holy Spirit that entrance He wanted into my heart and life. I no longer cared what other people would think. I was broken, but I was healing.

At some point in those years, despite his desperate and constant attempts to continue to control, dominate and manipulate me, despite his forceful, intimidation tactics and attacks against me, I grew stronger. My measure of truth was no longer the words that came out of his mouth. Oh, I would still catch myself saying, "But he said …" Thankfully I would at least recognize it now. His words, his threats, his actions would still throw me, but their impact was lessened--it was no longer paralyzing--and the effect did not last as long. I grew hopeful. I was finally able to turn my face to the sun, like my little flower (See Appendix 2) and be free.

[Journal entry from my most recent birthday. The contrast to the previous entries, even for me, is so remarkable, and so exciting!]

March 24, 2015

Happy Birthday! Everyday seems like my birthday as I walk with You! The joy, peace and confidence You have given me is incredible. You truly do put chaos back into order … You have blessed me with so much. I love my job, my kids, my walk with You, the excitement you are unfolding, my ministry teams, my friends, my house, my giftings, and especially my time with You, Lord. I have been thrilled getting to know the Father's heart. Thank you that I am in the center of Your will, and for the knowledge and power that flows because of it. Praise the Lord!

$\mathcal{H}$appy are those who hear the joyful call to worship,

for they will walk in the light of Your presence, LORD.

They rejoice all day long in Your wonderful reputation.

They exult in Your righteousness. You are their glorious strength.

Psalm 89:15

$\mathcal{F}$or I hold you by your right hand – I the LORD your God.

And I say to you, Don't be afraid. I am here to help you.

Isaiah 41:13

Dear Child,

Rest in My love, child. I am here with you. My love flows all around you. You are absorbing My softness and gentleness. My depth of love surrounds you. You feel it now. You understand it now. From it will flow my living waters to surround you. I will guide you. Have no fear. Step by step as always, my child. On this day, as on all days, My love pours out on you. You are My beloved. I dance with you as gently and softly as the spring rain. It falls all around you, filling you up, watering you with My tender mercies. It will fill your heart, your soul, every part of you, and soon flood into the lives of others. You are walking with Me, in My will. It is a joyous thing, a treasure for all to see. Share, My love, share. Teach, my love, teach. Rejoice, My love, rejoice. All is well. You draw your strength from Me. I will be here with you. Step by step we walk, leading captives free. Our hearts are locked, set in motion as one. The treasures in you spill forth as you have set your desires in Me. Your will has been released to Me, so we can flow together as one. Our hearts are locked. Thank you for your obedience. A surrendered heart … is such a gift. Go now, my child, in peace for the day, in joy, in hope, in faith, in love. All is well. Go now. Share My love, My hope, My joy.

♥ Jesus

Thank you for this beautiful birthday message, Lord! I love you so, so, so much!

♥ Calli

Part 2

My Healing
Journey

Author's Note - Prayer Section

At the end of each chapter, you will see a section for a prayer time and scripture reading. I did not write the prayers; I only had the honor of editing them. They were prayed over you, and over me, in the power of Holy Spirit, by a team of godly people. Many tears were shed in the process. They were shed for you, and for me. Many revelations were given into the heart and mind of you, the reader. The prayers are not just words. If they were, there would honestly be no point to this entire book. Through the prayers, there is power to change your life; not in your strength, but by the strength of Holy Spirit, by the power of the name of Jesus Christ, and by the love of God the Father.

Take time to meditate on them. Pray them more than once. Sometimes, as layers of trauma are removed and healing comes, more, and more will be opened up, which will allow for more, and more healing. Sometimes the pain and trauma go so deep that if it were all stirred up at once, it would be too much for us. So God will reveal things slowly, bit by bit, and bring healing to each layer, one at a time.

This allows you to go deeper and deeper as you get more, and more healing. Even if you think a part of the prayer does not apply to you, pray it anyhow. Sometimes we don't even realize some of the things that are holding us captive until they are released. Sometimes the things that need healing are very good at staying hidden. Please feel free to modify the prayers to meet your specific circumstances, and go off on "Holy Spirit rabbit trails" if that is where you feel you are being led. Holy Spirit can lead you to different things that need to be uncovered in your life. That is how even more freedom will come.

Speak the prayers out loud. There is power in speaking it out loud. Freedom comes by speaking it out and claiming it for your life. If you are not in a private place or the right frame of mind when you come to a prayer section, mark it and go on, but do come back to it at a later time, when you can come before God and pour out your heart. This is where the power lies. This is why I wrote the book. This is why I poured out my entire heart to you. There was no other reason, except to be used by God to help bring freedom to your life ... and the freedom lies in the prayers. I know the power of Holy Spirit will meet you as you humble yourself and go after God, through reading His word, and through the prayers--the ones He led us to pray.

I pray over you right now, that as you come before God for each of your prayer times, that there will be an open channel, from you to heaven, and that you will feel Holy Spirit in and over you as you pray. I come against any blocks set in place to try to thwart the good plans God has for your freedom as you pray what Holy Spirit has laid out before you. I pray that God hides you in the shelter of His wings and that He comforts you as you lay your heart bare before Him. I pray God's protection over you as you pray. I pray this in the mighty name of Jesus.

Prepare to be amazed, dear Reader. God wants to break the chains off of your life so that you can walk in complete freedom, peace, and joy. Why? Because God loves you ... He wants to show you just how much.

P.S. A huge "Thank You" to my prayer teams, for your time, your tears, and your willing hearts.

♥ Love in Christ, Calli

Strategic Survival

Living in abuse becomes a brutal game of strategic survival. It is completely exhausting having always to stay one step ahead of your counterpart. It is not just survival for your life, but survival to maintain your sanity, to maintain the core essence of who you are, and to maintain some aspects of a regular life, where a broken dish or a toilet seat left up is a very big deal.

For me, this led to becoming deceptive in some areas. Though I am not proud of it (and have since had to repent), I don't regret it. Though I'd never considered myself a frivolous spender, neither was I excessively thrifty, just nicely somewhere in the middle. However, during the marriage, even when I was working full-time, I was rarely allowed to spend any money. (I use the term *allowed* with the meaning that if I were allowed something, it would not cause a fight when I did it. If I was not allowed, when I did it … watch out!) This was somewhat ironic! One time when he got angry with me, somehow a big screen TV showed up to console him. More money went out each month to pay for his car lease then for the mortgage on our beautiful home with the triple car garage. If I spent too much on groceries, I would be sure to hear about it, whereas if he spent the same amount or more, he was amazed at how great he did with all the deals he'd found.

When I did assert some small bits of independence with my finances, I was met with verbal assaults such as this one:

"We are broke now, you idiot. F*** off. Drop dead. If this were a classroom, you'd be in the slow one. You just don't get it. You have to suffer. You have to lose the house. You have had it too good. You have to be humiliated. I will continue to humiliate you until you get the message. I'm glad there are no guns in the house; I'd probably shoot myself."

Needless to say, I became leery to buy even such simple things as a centerpiece for our coffee table. However, after too much of the contradictory unfairness of the situation, I began to do what I considered was standing up for myself, albeit in a small way. If I needed or wanted a new piece of clothing, I would buy it and hide it in my closet for a month or so. Then, when he noticed me wearing it, I could honestly say, "No, I have had it for a while, I just haven't worn it." That seemed to appease him for some reason.

Money was even tighter after I had my son and was no longer working. Of course, I realize a husband and wife should agree on purchases, and one should not go behind the other's back. However, since the only purchases we could agree upon were for him, I felt justified in doing the same when it came to something that I felt was important, such as my son's baby pictures. I went behind his back and ordered them without his permission … more deception. When it came time to pay for them, the only source of income I had available to me were small sporadic checks from the sale of teacher resource material that I had previously published and was still selling. Once he realized what I was doing, and that I had a separate bank account that he had forgotten about (which I do not regret having), it became a race to the post office to get the checks.

It was the same issue with my time. I could go to my job as a teacher without a problem, and perform any extracurricular duties that were required. Family functions were allowed as well, but he often did not attend them with me. Anything outside those areas was fair game for the battlefield. Events with friends were often sabotaged, or at the very least would bring on an onslaught of remarks focused on my selfishness and how I was not committed to the family. Other times he would say, "See you later, have fun!" You never knew quite what you would get on any given day.

Another frequent battle was his refusal--at times--to allow me to watch my school's sporting games. This was not a battle I was willing to lose. It was something that had been important to me since I began teaching and was key in relationship building with my students. To sidestep his controlling demands, I would tell him I had to go to school to do some work for report cards and then take my pile of correcting into the gym and mark while watching the game. It was deceptive, but I felt like I had to do such things to try and preserve some of the things that were important to me, instead of melting into the fractional shadow of a person that he wanted me to be.

When you read informational books on abuse, they often talk about being splintered as a person. This is exactly how it happens. Little bits of you are stripped away, one tiny piece at a time. Many of the things that were once so important to you, those things that make up your personality such as interests, opinions, time spent with people you enjoy, passions, and talents, become not worth the fight. You cannot fight for everything, and everything is such a battle. It is just too hard on you mentally, physically, and emotionally. It sucks everything out of you, as you may have to face days, weeks, months, or even years of torment for each thing you pick in which to stand your ground. Many of the things you stood up for in the beginning just don't seem worth it anymore. The world and its responsibilities do not stop just because you are emotionally drowning.

This splintering process had made its mark on me. I am an artist, yet the only painting of mine that was allowed on the wall was one I had made for Rob while we were dating. After our seven month separation, two of my watercolor paintings made it onto the living room wall. A little while later, though, after taking them down for some renovations, they never went back up. It was another part of me that was not worth the fight. I loved to read, but was constantly belittled for my choice of fiction over nonfiction. I still read, but not nearly as much. Again, parts of what make you an individual, you in your own right, are slowly and methodically chipped away. Worn and weary, it gets hard to keep standing. You have to choose your battles very carefully; more strategic survival.

This chaotic, never-ending game led me to become deceptive in other areas of my life as well. Feeling forced to hide the lie that was my life, I began to live in secrecy. Hiding the abuse, or at least certain aspects of it, became a conscious, although not an honest or wise, choice. When talking with my sister, I would often complain of some of the things that had recently been happening. After consoling me and giving me the indignation against him that I needed to hear, she would say, "Well, at least he is not getting physical anymore or then you'd have to leave again." It had, in fact, been physical on several occasions, but I chose to leave those parts out. In my distorted perspective back then, he had not quite crossed the moving line of physical abuse that I had predetermined would be my point of tolerance.

I just wasn't ready to leave. Deep down I felt that it was not worth me leaving and breaking up the family because of what seemed at the time, minor incidents of physical abuse that were occurring. Sometimes I wished he would just hit me hard in the face, even once, and that would give me the release I needed to leave. He never did; he would only grab my face or my throat. When he did hit me, it was always on the shoulder or in the ribs, and never full strength--just hard enough to hurt and get my attention without breaking any bones, (thus not crossing my line). He always managed, in a warped way, to somewhat restrain himself.

I remember one time being on the phone with my mom and feeling like I had to blatantly lie and say, "Yes, everything is fine." I knew in my heart that I would have to avoid seeing her for a while. The thumbprint bruise on my jaw was just too much of a telltale sign that all was not well, as I had professed.

This double life was the same with my friends. After our reconciliation from the seven-month separation, I became pregnant right away. I was thrilled, as this was a miracle in itself. I had polycystic ovaries and had been told it would be very difficult to have children. Besides, I thought, the change in his behavior after all these months of counseling was remarkable.

Once I had children my social world changed, and I made a whole new group of friends in the community in which I was living; people who knew nothing of my history. It was like we were given a new start. Within four months, despite the intense counseling, he reverted backward to his familiar patterns of behavior, and I was forced back into my normal unhealthy way of life. I was, however, not ready to let go of the sense of normalcy I had received from having a social life where people did not have to feel like they were holding their breath around me, fearing to ask me anything, or wondering what to say ... or not say. I felt it was safer this way, as again, I feared when people knew too much as they might slip up when he was around and say something that would prove to him that I was breaking his demand of "What happens behind closed doors, stays behind closed doors." My friends might also act awkward around him and thus tip him off. He was very perceptive and didn't miss much ... real or imagined ... then I would be in trouble! I also feared that if my new friends knew what was going on, what our lives were really like, they would be hesitant about socializing with us or allowing their kids to be involved in our lives. Consequently, a life of secrecy was again established.

Lying to my parents, avoiding things with my sister, being fake with my friends ... this was just not who I was or what I was about. What kind of person was I becoming? Where would this end? How was it a normal life to wish to be hit in the face by someone who was supposed to love, honor and cherish me? How distorted was I becoming? What kind of life was I living? How come he couldn't just "get it," and stop? What could I do to change it? Anything? What would happen if I left? Would it be over, or just worse--constantly looking over my shoulder in fear? What would life be like if I just up and ran away, taking my children far away and not telling anyone where we were going (to keep us safe), and start over? Would he leave me alone, or stop at nothing to hunt me down?

I often looked at the missing person photos on the wall at Walmart and noted when it was a mother who had "abducted" her children, thinking and hoping that she had made it; that she got out and was safe and was living somewhere in peace, joy and freedom. I wondered the same for myself ... Would I ever be able to live in peace, joy and freedom again? I eventually found that the answer is "Yes." It wasn't easy, but nothing in life that is worthwhile ever is.

When I started putting some of the pieces back together after I left, I found I had lost some of myself and could now understand when the media talked about "Finding Yourself." After all the searching, and some wrong roads and bad choices, I discovered the best way to find myself was to find God and to take care of me ... in that order. On the next few pages, I've described what I did to chase after God, but I did not do it all at once. It changed and grew with me, as I changed and grew. Everyone is different. You will need to find your own path. And it will change and grow as you change and grow. I hesitated to write this list, as I do not want it to become an overwhelming "to do" list that you feel you must accomplish in order to heal--especially for those of you who feel like you are already in over your head and treading water just to survive. Actually, God had asked me to ditch all the "to do" lists in my life for a season--and I lived by those lists! Instead of a "to do" list, these are things that God led me to do, one at a time, over a long period of time.

It was like a path of stepping stones was being laid out ahead of me. He would drop one specific thing in front of me, and I would do that, or go there, or change this ... and that would lead to the next thing, in its time. That is all I did. I took one step at a time, guided by the Lord. The emphasis was on being in the presence of God; not "doing," just "being." These are the things that gave me the opportunity to seek Him, and be in His presence.

These things might be new to you and even seem a little strange ... or maybe you already do some or many of them. Maybe

God will highlight one to you as you read through them, and you will feel this little tug in your spirit that maybe you are supposed to try it. Perhaps God will drop something totally different into your lap, and you experience a "knowing," that God wants you to do it. Everyone's journey is different. God is amazing like that!

For me, my journey looked like this:

1. **Put the big rocks in first**. This refers to doing the most important things in your day first. Then you will have time for some of the lesser things. Spending time with God regularly was the most powerful factor in my healing and my transformation. Everything else flowed out of this. Reading a devotional, responding to it in a journal, and writing out any scripture that seemed to jump off the page at me was crucial. I found that the journal helped keep my mind focused, and then I also had a record of any questions I had asked God, or concerns I faced. When these would be answered, I could go back in my journal and see what God had done! It took me a long time to get to this stage, however ... I wish I could have done it sooner, but maybe I was just not ready. Up until January 2015, my scattered devotional times seemed to be a one-way affair. But, inspired by my warrior friend who had regular conversations with God, I began to seek His voice during this time. I began to listen, really listen to God, and ask Him what He would say to me. Then I would write down anything I felt in my heart. It was altogether amazing to see my journey unfold; to see Him put the pieces together as my life and heart were transformed. This book was born out of my times with Him.

2. **Saturate yourself with God**. Listen to teachings and read books whenever you get the chance, but do it at a pace that suits you; do not let yourself get overwhelmed with "to read" or "to do" lists. I

started with Joyce Meyer, *Beauty for Ashes,* and Graham Cook. I played the teachings while I was doing dishes and cleaning my house. Also, attend church, retreats, and conferences that seem suitable for you at the time. Depending where you are in your journey, join ministry teams, and pray for others every chance you get.

3. **Praise God**! Be thankful in everything and for everything. Write down your praises--how God has answered prayers, but praise Him for who He is, as well. The book *Power in Praise,* by Merlin Carothers, provided a greater understanding of this and, therefore, was a turning point for me.

4. **Listen to the prompts of the Holy Spirit** and be obedient-- immediately if possible! More, and more will open up for you as your heart becomes more, and more obedient. He is looking for a faithful heart to use. It makes your walk with God more intimate, and there is much healing in this. This is a tough one to understand when you are in, or coming out of, a relationship with someone who is very controlling. A controlling person demands obedience for their own selfish, personal gain. God asks for obedience out of love and for your ultimate betterment. God is good and faithful. We can trust that He will not ask us to do anything that will harm us.

5. **Ask**! Ask for guidance and direction and for Him to give you the steps to your journey. We are each called to our own journey, so do not compare yourself with others. Do not worry where they are in their life. Focus on you and your family. God will show you as far ahead as you need to see; no more, no less!

6. **Seek** prophetic word if God brings you that opportunity. Record it and transcribe it. Keep it all together in a way that will preserve it and

make it accessible. Read it through as often as you need, gleaning the information from it that God wants to show you. You are given the words to show you where you are going. This helps you walk it out. Pray about it. Ask God for direction concerning your prophetic word. Ask Him for revelation if you are to do anything to work towards that area, and respond to what you learn! He is giving you this insight for a reason. Read it again as you go through different stages in your healing process, and new information will come to light.

7. **Take courses** that become available to help you heal. Contact your local church or search online for any healing courses that seem appropriate to your situation. Pray that God will provide and make a way for you to attend. The courses I took were Divorce Care, The Genesis Process, Cleansing Stream, (I was a participant for two years, then on the ministry team), Elijah House Trauma Course, and the Domestic Violence Course from Family Services.

8. **Find a prayer partner** or two or three! My prayer partners have had a huge impact on my life, both spiritually and emotionally. They give you that "shoulder to cry on" when you need it, and pour prayer into your life when you cannot necessarily do it on your own. Giving back to your partners also provides another aspect of your healing. I cannot even begin to describe the difference they have made in my life.

9. **Play worship music** in your house continually. This changes the atmosphere. Choose songs that speak to your heart and listen to them over and over. They seem to become prophetic in your life. (Or maybe they are prophetic in your life ... that is why they touch you ... I haven't figured that out yet!)

10. **Be purposeful**, mindful and intentional in what you choose to do, and where and with whom you choose to spend your time. Realign your priorities as often as you need.

The second priority in your healing journey is YOU! Yes, you. Dear Reader, please take care of yourself! This is such a difficult time for you. We used to joke with each other at the domestic violence course, about how it was a good day if you brushed your teeth! Please do what you can to take care of yourself. Becoming healthy includes body, soul (mind, will, and emotions) and spirit. Do what you can in each stage of your journey but please remember, if you and your health are always at the bottom of the list of your priorities ... who will take care of you if you don't take care of yourself ... who will take care of those around you if you are unable to because you haven't taken care of yourself? I learned that the hard way for a while. Make yourself a priority--even over your children if needed--if you are not healthy, neither will they be healthy.

Do everything you can to educate yourself on your situation. Read books, watch videos and shows, and research websites on domestic violence, abuse, narcissism, borderline personality disorder, antisocial personality disorder, healing trauma, dealing with anger, grieving, and anything else that is relevant to you and your experiences. I found Patricia Evans and Lundy Bancroft were particularly informative authors.

Remember dear Reader, God loves you for who you are right now, not for who you should be, who you will be or who you used to be, but exactly for who you are right now. He loves everything about you. You need to fall in love with yourself too ... the you who God created ... with all of your giftings, talents and shortcomings. So get to know yourself, and begin to enjoy your own company if you do not do so already.

Do things you love! Take a bath with candlelight and music. Play a sport. Paint a picture. Find a hobby that you are passionate about and do it often, without any guilt. Go for a walk on the beach or in the park. Make a weekly date with a friend. Get a pet. Spoil yourself during the entire month of your birthday! Surround yourself with things you find uplifting and peaceful. Stencil some encouraging words and scriptures on your walls and write them on the mirror. Read them often and learn to live by them. Get excited about your life. Learn to honor your body exactly as it is by eating healthy and exercising regularly. Clip out encouraging articles and pictures and post them on your fridge. Develop your giftings. Take a class. Spoil the important people in your life, letting them know what treasures they are to you. This can be healing for all of you. Please, dear Reader, do whatever it takes to learn to enjoy life again ... there is so much to live for.

The first step in sorting out the chaos is to ask God to take control of your life whether it is for the first time, or if you need to recommit to Him for a brand new start in life.

Please pray this prayer with me. It will change your life.

Salvation Prayer/Recommitment Prayer

> I feel my heart stir God, and I know You are real and that You are my only hope to chase away the darkness. I know You want to do something in my life. You came, and You died on the cross for me. You saved me from all my sins. Jesus, I want to stop the life I have been living. I want to turn and follow the King of Kings and the Lord of Lords. Jesus, be my Savior. Be my Lord. Be my salvation. I want to be a child of the living God. I was created for more than this, I know that, God. I want to serve You, the living God. Holy Spirit bring revelation to my heart and my mind. Wash me, cleanse me, and fill me with Your Holy Spirit. I pray this in Jesus' name. Thank You, Lord, for the new life you have given me, and the new creation You have made me.
>
> Amen.

I will now stand with you as you ask God for help in moving forward with your life, instead of just surviving it.

Thank You, Lord, that You are calling me back to life. Living in abuse is a type of death to so many things ... the death of who I was, death to my dreams, death to my perspectives on life ... I feel dead in so many ways. I thank You that You are here with me and You are weeping over me. I know You care even more than I do about what I've suffered. Thank You that You are calling me back to the newness of life and that my life can be even better than the life I dreamed for myself--which seems impossible to me, Lord, but I know that You can do the impossible. God, getting there is not easy. It can seem overwhelming, like having this gigantic "to-do" list of all the things I need to do to heal when I struggle sometimes to get through even the basics of life. So, God, I thank You that You will put the things I need to do in front of me, like bread crumbs along a path through the woods. I thank You that You will lead me to one thing, and that will open the door for something else, which will lead me to the next thing. I don't have to figure it all out or muster up anything to do it all on my own, but I just have to trust in Your guidance. Thank You that You do that for me, Lord. I thank You that these things are not just items to check off of a list, but they are opportunities to get to know You better, Lord, and that is what this is all about--getting to know You better and getting to know myself again. Thank You that You are making me new, making everything beautiful in its time, and for the hope You are restoring in me. God, I just thank You that You want me to be whole. I have lost so much of myself. So many parts of me have been splintered, fractured, and stolen from me by the enemy. God, I thank You that You want to restore all the lost parts of me.

You want to collect all that has been scattered and weave them together into something new. You are a God of redemption and You redeem all things Lord, so even though I know I won't be the same as before, I trust that I will be even better--my scars will show me that in You, I am wiser and stronger than I was before. I call all those pieces of myself back, and I give You permission to change them in any way that You need, to recreate me into who You want me to be. Thank You for making me whole.

Thank You, Lord, that You want me to live in the light and walk in the truth. I am sorry for the times I felt I had to lie and deceive to protect myself, my children, or someone else in my life. God, sometimes the people in the Bible and history told "good lies," and that seemed to be honored by You. But I can't always discern what a "good lie" is and what is not, so I repent of what was not honorable to You. I also repent for the lies and the deception I perpetuated out of fear, or otherwise, that perhaps unknowingly contributed to me being held in captivity. Lord, I lay it all down at Your feet. Take this burden from me.

God, please help me to walk in truth and integrity when I am in dangerous situations. Show me how to walk this treacherous path without getting trapped in deception. I ask for Your wisdom, Lord. Please give me the faith I need this day, to surrender to You completely. Lord, when You ask me to obey You it is not out of selfish desire or with the purpose of controlling me. Help me trust that it is out of love and mercy. There is absolutely nothing that You need from me. There is nothing I can do for You to make things better for You.

Everything You ask of me is for my benefit. Help me trust in Your goodness and Your wisdom for knowing what I need, even more than I do. Help me trust that You, who gave me all things, even Your own Son, will give me everything I need to live the life that You are calling me to live. This is Your promise to me. So I thank You that I can live in total surrender and obedience to you, Lord. Help me understand my new relationship with You as a daughter of the King; one who has a place in the kingdom, is protected and provided for, is loved, nurtured and cherished by her Father. Thank You, Lord, for what You want to do in me and through me. I pray all this in the mighty name of Jesus Christ.

Amen

*F*or I can do everything through Christ, who gives me

strength.

Philippians 4:13

*F*or nothing is impossible with God.

Luke 1:37

T rust in the Lord and do good. Then you will live safely in the land and prosper. Take delight in the Lord, and he will give you your heart's desires. Commit everything you do to the Lord. Trust him, and he will help you. He will make your innocence radiate like the dawn, and the justice of your cause will shine like the noonday sun.

Psalm 37:3-6

T hose who live in the shelter of the Most High will find rest in the shadow of the Almighty. This I declare about the Lord: He alone is my refuge, my place of safety; he is my God, and I trust him. For he will rescue you from every trap and protect you from deadly disease. He will cover you with his feathers. He will shelter you with his wings.

His faithful promises are your armor and protection.

Psalm 91:1-4

> *T*hen I will rejoice in the Lord. I will be glad because he rescues me. With every bone in my body I will praise him: "Lord, who can compare with you? Who else rescues the helpless from the strong? Who else protects the helpless and poor from those who rob them?"
>
> *Psalm 35:9-10*

Dear Child,

Fear not, I am with you all days, when you are weak and when you are strong. Let Me be your strength on the days when you are weak. Those are precious--I treasure those days when you call on Me to be your strength. I battle for you. I am your shield. I welcome you into My presence; into the light of My love for you. My peace goes before you. My shield is strong when you are weak. When you have need of Me, that is when I am so close beside you, holding your hand. Let Me be beside you. Let Me walk beside you, strengthening you. My peace goes with you. My joy goes with you even--and more so--on those days.

♥ Jesus

Don't Feed the Bear!

DON'T FEED THE BEAR!

    Yes, Lord, but didn't you see how he…

DON'T FEED the bear!

    Yes, Lord, but how come…

DON'T feed the bear.

    Yes, Lord, but…

Don't feed the bear.

[Deep breath.]

[Heavy sigh.]

    Yes, Lord.

Don't feed the bear, my child.

    Yes, Lord.

I was blessed beyond measure to have the senior pastor of what became my home church be one of the first pillars in my healing. Without even knowing me, he phoned me at the request of my sister-in-law, who attended his church. For years after that initial phone call, he poured into our marriage. Then, after Rob's final resistance to submit his will to God, he continued to pour into my life. Early on, when there was cooperation in counseling, Rob and I would laugh at how the pastor must have our house bugged; he always managed to call and check on us right at the point of escalation. There was so much wisdom he instilled in me over the years (I could write a book on that alone!), but two things that still stand out the most, are the "Hospital Bed" and the "Don't Feed the Bear" analogies.

After I had left Rob for the final time, I was being pushed and pulled to make a decision. Was I going to "tear this family apart" or "put this thing back together?" When I felt myself cracking from the pressure of being forced to make a decision that I was not mentally, emotionally, or even physically able to make, the pastor would come to my rescue and remind both Rob and me that it was like I was lying in a hospital bed with a broken back. I did not have to--rather *could not*--start, on either journey, but needed to focus all my energy into healing. I had to heal physically, mentally and emotionally, before I could make any serious decisions or start moving in any specific direction. Trusting this wisdom from God took all the pressure off of me. It freed me from all guilt of doing what I had to do for myself and instead allowed God to heal me. With a broken back, no one--not even yourself--can have any expectations of you to start walking anytime soon. Though I still would receive that pressure to make decisions, I trusted that the pastor had heard from the Lord, and I was just to rest, heal, and grow closer to Jesus.

The other revelation that had a huge impact on my healing journey and who I came to be, was the wisdom to not "Feed the Bear." Often, as the pastor counseled me, he would remind me of this.

Then, as I was facing different circumstances the Lord would remind me too, that I was not to "Feed the Bear." Feeding the bear would equate with dwelling on any thoughts, feelings or words that would build up the anger, jealousy, vengeance or bitterness against someone that could eventually become rooted in my own heart and cause me to become angry, jealous, vengeful and bitter. Any words of hate, complaining about tough circumstances instead of being grateful, jealous thoughts, vengeful thinking, or other such things, would all feed the bear. This would cause that bear to grow, and eventually overtake all my right attitudes and harden my soft heart, making me into a person I did not want to be; one with whom God would not be pleased, nor could He use. There would be no beauty for ashes, but instead, just more ashes.

For me to become healthy and whole and walk in the joy, peace and freedom I now walk, I couldn't afford to feed the bear. I would catch myself doing so, as unfair circumstances would rise time, and time again. But then those words would rise in my spirit, and as unjustly as I felt I was being treated, I knew the thoughts--if I let them churn around in my head and heart for any length of time--would begin to destroy me and take with it all hope for a prosperous soul in my future, and that of my kids. Many, many times those words would echo loudly and firmly in my brain, and I would eventually submit. Soon, those words would have to be only whispered to my heart, and I would be obedient; I continue to be obedient even today.

Though I still get accused of being a "vengeful, vindictive, bitter, divorced woman," deep in my soul I know the truth. God has saved me from that road. All bitterness and anger has been, and is being, surrendered unto the Lord; I do not have to carry it with me. I will not carry it with me. I will not pass it down to my children. It was finished at the cross, and I am free to be the woman God has called me to be. Let me walk that path with you as you call on God to help you make that choice of freedom.

Heavenly Father,

I come before You with my heart in my hands. I lift it up to You. I pray that by the power of Your Holy Spirit, You would cause faith to rise in my heart, and I would be able to trust You with my whole situation, with my whole life, and with all my circumstances, as unlovely as they are. Lord, I put them all into Your hands. I pray You help me to walk the path of freedom and new life. Help me to take every thought captive to the obedience of Christ. I pray, Father, that You grant me a special grace to discipline my mind not to meditate or focus on all the ugly, negative things that have happened. Keep me from dwelling on the things that were said to me or done to me, or on any other of the negative circumstances of my life that I never believed would ever happen to me. They have happened, and now they are trying to hold me captive and keep me from the life you desire me to have--that You have designed for me--one of freedom and joy, hope, and laughter, love and peace. You see all these things, Lord, and You know them all, and You will carry them all for me--I don't have to anymore. So by the power of Holy Spirit, I release all these negative events in my life to You and I put my trust in You. Renew my mind. Inspire thoughts of forgiveness, mercy, grace, trust and faith in my mind. Replace any thoughts of jealousy, vengeance, ungratefulness, anger, and bitterness, with thoughts about You, Lord--about how much You love me, how much You are for me, and that You have a wonderful plan and destiny for my life.

I pray, Lord, that all my negative thoughts are replaced by positive thoughts, about what You have in store for me, and my amazing new future in You, full of freedom, peace and hope. I pray, Lord, for Your healing grace. Heal my mind and heal my heart. Wash them clean. Purify them. I pray that You restore my joy and let it overflow like a fountain, into the lives of all those around me. I pray that right now, by the power of Your Holy Spirit, You give me the supernatural strength I need to cast down every negative thing and to take every thought captive to the obedience of Christ. Father, let Philippians 4:8 be my portion, that whatever is pure, whatever is lovely, whatever is worthy of praise, that my mind will dwell on these things, Lord. I need special strength to do that, as I cannot do it on my own. I praise You and thank You for what You are going to do in my life. Thank you for releasing the power of Holy Spirit to help me grow in grace and love. I pray all these things in Jesus' name.

Amen

Look after each other so that none of you fails to receive the grace of God. Watch out that no poisonous root of bitterness grows up to trouble you, corrupting many.

Hebrews 12:15

> *A*nd now, dear brothers and sisters, one final thing. Fix your thoughts on what is true, and honorable, and right, and pure, and lovely, and admirable. Think about things that are excellent and worthy of praise.
>
> *Philippians 4:8*

Dear Child,

My peace surrounds you. Drink it in. Be filled deeply by it. It will give you strength for the day. For My day. A day for loving Me. A day for following Me. A bright, shining day where you can love others and glorify Me. A day worth living. A day filled with peace and joy if you let it. I am here with you always, in all you do. I am surrounding you. I am your breath. Your breath is in Me and Mine is in you. Drink this in. Let it flow out of you. Let it flow from you, surround you, overtake you. I am with you in all you do. Do each task with peace and joy, knowing that I am guiding you, giving you energy, divine wisdom, and grace. My grace abounds. It flows out of you if you let it. Be graceful in all you do. As I have given you grace, such grace, give it to others. Hear My voice of peace. Hear My voice of love. It is reaching out to you. You will find it in all you do if you seek it, look for it, thrive upon it. I am with you in all you do, all you say. Glorify Me in all you do, in all you say. I am with you. My divine power reaches out to all those who seek. Ask and it is yours. All I have is yours, just as all you have is Mine. Trust Me. Depend on Me. Rely on Me. That is your truth. That is your walk. That is Me.

♥ Jesus

Just a Little Angry

[This is a journal entry, written several years after I had left. It was in response to a letter that Rob had given me that shows he attempted to see some of the things that happened in our marriage from what he thought was my perspective. But, it angered me, as I felt it barely even scraped the surface of all I went through. I felt it was minimized greatly, and did not even begin to address the level of trauma I faced in our marriage.]

I don't know what I feel about "the letter."

It was a pretty tamed down version of my life.

Come on 'hun,'

Where are the c's and b's and of course the many f's?

Where were the threats on my body, my life, my very being?

Where was the bruise on my arm, my face, my neck?

The kids ... who witnessed and experienced more than their poor little hearts can take ...What about them?

Yeah, pretty tame version of my so called life, sucked of all vitality,

My drama that YOU made it:

BUT NOT THE HORRID, INTANGIBLE EXISTENCE THAT WAS MY LIFE –

Not the intensity of hell I walked through every day.

Where was the fear, the humiliation, the criticism,

The absolute cutting to the core of every part of me,

Of every facet of my being which you systematically attacked with cold, calculating precision,

Meant to destroy me, my life, my love, my spirit, my very soul?

Where is that hate that looked at me with disgust and contempt,

Trying to persuade me into believing I could do nothing right,

Trying to bleed me into believing I was the pathetic one.

Yes, the events were partially accurate,

But you still cannot face the WHOLE TRUTH.

You could not bring yourself to write it.

You opened the door, and yes, you even looked in from my perspective ...

But you have not crossed through.

You have the images, but have not felt the dread, the trepidation with which I had to tread

To save myself, save the children.

We had everything, yet we, the kids and I, were forced to suffer.

And for what?

There was no accident, no illness.

We were not poor, we did not want for food, a job, for anything material.

There was no horrible situation that caused it.

It was by your hand, your choice, you imposed it on us.

And for what?

Why did you choose to hold your family, your wife, captive for so many, many years?

We could have had it all.

We did have it all.

And you chose to destroy it,

Destroy it all.

You had your second chance, and your third, your fourth, and fifth.

So many, many chances to save your family, save yourself.

Now you understand? Is that what you are trying to say?

Now you get it?

Now you know you can't throw your wife into the wall?

Now you know it's not O.K.?

Yeah, and MAYBE you shouldn't have gotten so creative with the ways

To degrade and belittle her?

What? Every name in the book wasn't awful enough on its own?

The c's just weren't sufficient to put her in her place?

Yeah and the control and manipulation;

You shouldn't have been quite so forceful, maybe not create the sheer terror to control?

There are more subtle ways in which to control.

There's always money, sex and emotion.

Oh yeah, you used those too.

So, what are you saying by your letter?

That you have come to your senses?

That you have seen what you have done?

That NOW you realize it was wrong?

How could you NOT know it was wrong?

All of it.

How could you not know?

How is it NOT possible to know?

It was not O.K.

I took it.

I took it all, for the family.

But now I left for the family.

To save the family.

We cannot be with someone who does not know, does not know

Without having to go through this all,

That it is wrong to do the things you did, to say the things you said.

Which is worse?

That you knew you were doing it;

It was done on purpose,

Cruel and calculating.

Or that you knew you were doing it, but could not control yourself,

Showing how deep and stagnant your issues run.

Or that you didn't know,

Weren't conscience of the depth of your brutality;

A character flaw so deep

I do not believe it can be changed.

So which is it?

Which scenario are you going to claim?

So yes, your letter reflects a glimpse of our tragic lives together,

But that is all, a reflection, touching the surface.

It is NOT EXPOSED, EXPLICIT and RAW,

Like the TRUTH of us.

(I will not share this with you, because sharing this is sharing my soul, And I WILL NOT LET YOU IN.)

Wow. As I read that, I know it came straight from my heart at the time. It fed the bear. I was definitely angry! Thankfully I couldn't write that now if I tried, and for that, I am grateful. I think I needed the anger at the time, to stand strong as he pushed hard against me, trying to force and guilt me into old familiar patterns. I needed that anger to help me, as my sister said, "Build my fences and stand my ground."

I know if I held onto that kind of anger, it would have eaten my soul. I would eventually be no different than the pawns of the enemy who perpetuate this human destruction. I had to release it; have to release it … and will have to keep releasing it into the hands of my Savior. I do this physically, taking my offense and symbolically putting it into my upturned hands, then lifting them up and saying "Lord, I give this to you. Take it from me. It is yours." God then asks me to walk through the forgiveness, time, and time again, following each wave of injustice. I walk quickly and easily into forgiveness now, but it wasn't always so. It took me years (and a stubborn prayer partner) to understand that to forgive is to forgive. It is not trusting someone undeserving of trust, but trusting Jesus. Forgiveness does not mean they have gotten away with it or that it was justified. No! Forgiveness simply releases them into the hands of God to take care of it. He is far more capable of handling it than I, and it releases me to heal.

It took some time to stop the numbness and start feeling, allowing myself to walk through the pain, and to cry the cleansing tears that were necessary. I had to allow the anger and the grief to rise, and then surrender them unto God … then surrender them unto God … then surrender them unto God. Layer upon layer, each level went deeper and deeper into my heart until I did not think I could even bear it anymore. At times, I was not ready. Other times the trauma went too deep, and I would shut down. I remember running out of the room at a Cleansing Stream Retreat, while I was being prayed for saying, "I can't do this!" Another time at the same retreat, I was just so shut down, and nothing would come out of my mouth. The team leader, always hearing from the Spirit and usually relentless, just walked away saying, "Maybe you are not ready yet." I was shocked, but she knew that it was not the time to push--even gently. Nevertheless, God would bring it all up again, slowly. Piece by piece He would reveal things to my heart, in different ways, with different people surrounding me to help me through it. Then I had to forgive, first in obedience of the mind and will. The heart did not agree. But God honored that, and the heart soon followed. I had truly forgiven and doing so released me to heal.

As I held unforgiveness in my heart, it was like it consumed all the space. There was little room for anything else, like joy, freedom or peace. Once it was removed, though, God cleansed and healed my heart and replaced the now empty places with all the good things He had for me. It is amazing. He showed me that to the depths of your heart that you were cut open, that is to the depths of your heart His healing can go, and to that depth He can place His love, His joy, and His passion.

I feel more alive, more vibrant, more in love with God, with my kids, and with my life in all capacities, than I ever have--even before my years of trauma. Though I would not want to walk through what I have walked through again, at the same time, I would not replace the relationship that was forged with the Father because of it. And that is sensational. That is glorious.

Let me stand by you as you pray to obtain His glorious freedom!

Lord,

I come before You in total honesty and complete vulnerability. I know that only You can identify with this pain and anger that I am walking through because You walked it too. Sometimes, Lord, I feel like I live in a glass house, where I can look out and see life going on and others look in, and think my life is going fine. But there is a distortion: they might think they understand, but don't. So, in Jesus' name, I cut off any mocking spirit that says, "I understand," when they don't, or any other lies it speaks. I have been lied to, hurt and given false promises too many times, which has brought in fear and left me unable to trust anyone--even You, Lord. So in Jesus' name I break the vows I have made over my life that say I cannot trust anyone so that I am free to trust You and others. I want to love the way You love and see others the way You see them, but I cannot do it in my strength. Help me, Lord. Help me to forgive those that have harmed me.

I take authority over the spirit of anger. I ask that today, by the power of the blood of the Lamb, You would seal off the open door where the enemy has had access to bring pain, sorrow, shame and any form of anger into my life to degrade me. I place the cross of Christ between me and every form of anger and abuse that has been set against me. Lord, where anger has lodged deep within my soul and spirit, and in every way that anger has manifested in my body, my mind, my emotions and my spirit, I ask that it would be shut down, bound and gagged in the name of Jesus.

I take authority over every way that it is trying to manifest in the words I speak, my thoughts, and my actions. Lord, I pray that You would take them, and You would cleanse them. I pray that every way that anger has manifested itself in self-hatred and anger toward myself, resentment, and fear, be cut off. I pray that where anger has injured my spirit, where the words spoken over me have crushed me, that Your Spirit would cover me and You would revive every part of my broken spirit. Breathe life into my very being.

I pray that every time anger has stepped in to protect me, that it would be replaced with Your protection, Father. Disarm the anger. Lord, I pray that You instead would be my buffer, my strength, and my portion, my very present help in time of need, my strong tower where I can run to, and my identity.

Like the protection offered by a one-way mirror at a police station, where victims can identify the perpetrator without being seen, as I step forward and identify my wounds and the people and the things that have hurt me, I know you too are protecting me. I don't have to hide any longer behind anger, fear, and unforgiveness. You, Lord, are my one-way mirror. Even when I feel I cannot see You, You are there, and You see me. I thank You that You are protecting my heart and my family and that You will do a healing deep within me. Lord, with You protecting me I no longer have to be the victim, but I can walk in victory. I break off the victim spirit, through which I have been harmed. I do not walk in the spirit of defeat but by the power of Holy Spirit I can be an overcomer. I will overcome all the pain and destruction that has happened in my life.

Lord, there are places where my emotions may have been stunted or broken when I was not loved nor honored, nor treated as a woman or as a spouse, but as a child being reprimanded. So I call out a healthy emotional state for me, and I ask that You would bring complete healing to those emotions. Lord, I release the trauma of everything I have been through, emotionally and physically, to You. I ask that You restore me to my original design right down to the cellular level. For every internal cell that was under the vibration of anger, almost like it was ready to explode, I command it to stop in the name of Jesus. I ask that Your healing would come and You re-vibrate every cell in my body to that perfect vibration You created me to have; that vibration of healing, health, peace, love, joy, self-discipline, and faithfulness--all those gifts You placed within me. Restore Your perfect vibration to every cell in my body so that it would come into perfect alignment again.

Lord, You came to give freedom and free choice, so in the name of Jesus I also break off the spirit of control and manipulation that likes to tie itself to anger, to get what it wants, how it wants it. I cut off every way that anger has affected me in the principle of sowing and reaping. Every way that anger has sown something harmful into me, or that I sowed into others when I walked in anger, I pray that it would be not reaped in my life nor the life of my children or others around me. I cut that off now, Lord Jesus.

God, I also pray that where anger has been distorted, You would bring it into perspective and give me a healthy anger that would not be robbed by fear. When those feelings of righteous anger rise, I pray that fear would not cause me to pull back.

Instead, help me to press into the healthy anger that You provide for me to become a warrior and fight the enemy of my soul on my behalf, and on the behalf of others. I pray in Your name that You would bring my spirit into alignment with Yours to tear down every plan and tactic of the enemy. Jesus, I pray that there would be a healthy tenacity that rises to fight, that feels safe, and that the righteous anger that You designed me to have would not be quenched. Wake up the warrior in me, Lord!

Thank You that I am now free to walk in the spirit of truth, peace and freedom. The chains are broken. Thank You that I have been set free.

Amen

*U*nderstand this, my dear brothers and sisters: You must all be quick to listen, slow to speak, and slow to get angry. Human anger does not produce the righteousness God desires.

James 1:19-20

And "don't sin by letting anger control you." Don't let the sun go down while you are still angry, for anger gives a foothold to the devil.

Ephesians 4:26-27

Don't be misled – you cannot mock the justice of God. You will always harvest what you plant. Those who live only to satisfy their own sinful nature will harvest decay and death from that sinful nature. But those who live to please the Spirit will harvest everlasting life from the Spirit. So let's not get tired of doing what is good. At just the right time we will reap a harvest of blessing if we don't give up.

Galatians 6:7-9

> Get rid of all bitterness, rage, anger, harsh words, and slander, as well as all types of evil behavior. Instead, be kind to each other, tenderhearted, forgiving one another, just as God through Christ has forgiven you.
>
> *Ephesians 4:31-32*

Dear Child,

Rest in Me. Relax. Feel My peace. You need that to strengthen you. You will hear My voice clearly as you allow My peace to flood your soul, flood your heart, flood your mind. I am everything. You need Me to strengthen you. Then you will be healed. Do not try to grasp for more than you can handle. I am enough. Rest in My peace. Let it flow out of you. Let the sadness flow out of you and be released into My loving care. That can be achieved by trusting Me with your pain; letting Me into your heart to touch the deep places of pain that you still have kept hidden. The ones that are overtaking you still, and keep you from breathing. There is a happy ending. There is a win. You win with Me. Your life, your journey is a success, with Me being the prize. I am the goal. I am the light at the end of the tunnel. It is Me you seek. I am the treasure. How can you not win when you have found Me? My grace, My love, and My peace will radiate from you, and others will see and be drawn to Me through you. That is the treasure. It all flows out of Me. There is no other. I am the hope of salvation, but the hope of this life as well.

♥ Jesus

Abandoned

Confusion, doubt, guilt, insecurity, disbelief, anguish ... they all resulted from being abandoned. During my healing journey, it was difficult at first to make the connection between some of my experiences and the issue of abandonment. I had a solid upbringing, with my parents always being there for me. I had mistakenly believed that no one had left me. Even in the marriage I was the one who left. Consequently, I wondered, how could I possibly be dealing with the ramifications of being abandoned? In reality, I was abandoned, time, and time again. Abandonment comes in many forms. You can be abandoned without anyone ever physically leaving you.

For me, most of it played out in similar scenarios. I would be on holidays, and Rob would go to work. When I asked him to take some time off so that we could do something together, or as a family, he adamantly would reply that he had to work, usually throwing in a derogatory comment or two about the level of my intelligence. No holidays would be taken, no trips, no events, no days at the beach with the kids, no visiting, no weekend getaways (other than the rare, disastrous camping weekend), no special times or special memories would be made. I was ignored and on my own, both before and after kids, for the entire stint of my vacations. However, the very day I was to return to work, whether it was a day, week or two months I had been off, he would beg me to take some time off. Maybe "drop the kids off at your parents and we can fly to New York ..." It was always right now; never with any advanced notice so I could plan ahead and make it work for us.

When this first started to happen, I felt guilty that I could not just take that day or week off with only a moment's notice, and go off with him. It just does not work like that when you are a teacher--and a mother. Those things have to be planned ahead of time and applied for through the school board. I would be dumbfounded … completely unable to figure out the logistics of his rational. "Why would he … why couldn't he … It would be so easy for him to …" His way of thinking did not make sense to me. His schedule was totally flexible; mine was totally set. He could easily have made them match. To me, that was just logical for a married couple. Nevertheless, it continued to happen year, after year, after year, no matter what I said or what I did. Furthermore, the blame and guilt would be shifted onto me, time and time again, about how I wasn't committed to him and how I wouldn't make the necessary sacrifices to spend time with him, or do things with him.

As I began to realize what was happening, the confusion, shock, and disbelief melded into insecurity; feelings of worthlessness and hopelessness settled in. This act seemed like a physical confirmation of his statements like "Being with an educated woman is a waste of time," or "You bore me to tears," and "everything you know is boring." It dragged me to a place of deep sadness. Despair filled the pit of my belly. I was alone. Married, but utterly alone and abandoned.

Other small but constant incidents also fed into these feelings of abandonment. During our rare attempts at camping trips, he would start a fight while we were packing up. It gave him an excuse to sit at the picnic table, coffee in hand, and watch me contemptuously as I was left to do the entire takedown and pack up on my own. Or, he would become upset about something or other, related to me or not, making him pull away and hibernate and leave me to wander and explore by myself. Again, I was left alone in a beautiful place where we could be having so much fun and enjoying life! Another time, near the beginning of our marriage, we were at a storage facility trying to deal with my things as we moved into our new house. I had furniture that was important to me, like my grandparents' old metal bed frame that I had refinished. He became angry about having to deal with too much stuff, threw it all out on the ground, and left. Thankfully I had my own vehicle with me, but again I was left to deal with everything on my own.

I also faced financial abandonment. For example, I had received a small inheritance from my grandparents and wanted to put some of it aside to pay my upcoming tax bill. He persuaded me to use all the inheritance money to pay down our debt instead, and he would help me deal with the tax bill when it came. That is sound advice in normal circumstances. When my tax bill came, I went into debt to pay it. He refused to help.

Often he would leave the house and refuse to tell me where he was going or when he was coming back, and other times he would not come home after work at all. On one occasion, I learned that he had checked into a hotel. I had been worried about him all night. He wanted to give me "a dry run at single parenting," to be sure I knew how it felt. In this, and in many other such circumstances, I was left stranded and fending for myself--emotionally and physically abandoned.

It became so discouraging, as these sad scenarios replayed on a continuous and unending loop in different variations, but always with the same result. Alone; I was always alone no matter what I did. I started to ask myself what I had done that was so terrible to get sentenced to a life of such isolation and loneliness. Was I ever going to not feel like this? Would I always feel so alone in the world with no hope of it changing? Would I have to do everything, face everything, deal with everything, and fight every battle, alone?

I thank God for my friends and family who would help me as much as they could. Even so, I was left to face too many things on my own. Living in secrecy made things worse, as I often felt I could not ask for the needed help. To combat this, I would shore myself up mentally just to survive and to keep moving forward. I took on an attitude of independence, of rigidity; building huge walls that would tower over me to keep me held up, strong, hard, and tough. My walls said, "I can do this. I don't need anyone. I will survive. You can't touch me." However they also said, "I can't let you in, or I might get hurt, or fall apart. If I let go of my walls, everything will come crashing down. Without my walls, I would be alone and afraid." Tragically, my walls almost destroyed my relationship with my sister who was desperately trying to reach out to me. My walls kept me from healing and from really living or knowing who I was.

I began to scream in my spirit. "I CAN'T KEEP WALKING LIKE THIS! PLEASE HELP ME! SOMEBODY HELP ME." My walls would not let anyone in. They couldn't let anyone in. It was hard to keep a soft heart when it kept getting stepped on. My walls kept my heart safe. Even after leaving the abusive relationship my walls were solidly in place. They had been built up so strong; reinforced by every incident. They were not going anywhere.

You cannot heal your heart if you do not expose it. Your heart cannot be touched until you allow it--surrender it. Thankfully, God is gentle and merciful. He walked me ever so slowly through this one. With each course, each prayer time, each worship time, each new Godly relationship, God would slowly melt away a little more of my walls. As I pressed in (see Strategic Survival), I allowed God to touch and heal more, and more of my heart. I could feel His love pouring in through the little cracks that were being formed within my walls.

The most remarkable part of this process happened at a Cleansing Stream Retreat. I was up in the prayer line, and I knew God wanted to do another layer of deep healing, but I was fighting it. My walls still supplied that hard edge to me that kept me from releasing everything. But God is relentless in His pursuit of us. So was K, one of the ministry leaders. She could see I was internally fighting to keep everything inside of me together. Thankfully, that is not what God wants. He wants us to let it all go; release it all into His hands and let Him carry us and our burdens. K showed me a statue she had brought to the retreat that weekend. It was a statue of a man being held in Jesus' outstretched arms. The look on the man's face was incredible. The look portrayed something beyond going from anguish to peace; it was total, absolute surrender. Surrender of everything--every part of him into His Lord's arms. I looked at the man's face, said, "Oh no," and broke down into tears. Guided by Holy Spirit, K stepped behind me and asked me to physically surrender and lay back in her arms. She wanted me to live that experience of total surrender. I resisted at first, but then something inside of me broke. I surrendered all into my Savior's arms. I felt the peace of sweet release flood my soul, and I knew God had done a deep work of healing in my heart.

Since then, little by little, He has continually brought up specific areas of my life and has asked me to surrender them to Him. He is never forceful or demanding of it. God is a gentleman. As you open yourself up to Him and take another step of faith, He blesses you time, and time again. He heals you time, and time again. He loves and encourages you time, and time again. His loving kindness allows you to open yourself up to Him and be vulnerable. It is not something we have to force or defend ourselves against. Rather, it is like being led gracefully along the right path of healing.

There is peace in this. He, who sees the whole picture, can take care of everything--everything we give Him--so much better than we can. When He asked me to surrender my children to Him, in my mind, I put them in my hands and offered them up. He put them on a swing and lowered them back down to me so I could play with them. My life, my health, my healing, my friends, my career, my future, my finances, my house, my crazy schedule, even my cats, have all been surrendered to my Lord. Instead of building walls of protection, I have learned to turn to God to keep me safe. I have learned to trust Him. I trust He has a plan for my life, and I trust that the plan is good. That way, things can still get in and out of my heart and touch me. I can feel things and not just be totally numb to everything around me as I was when I fought to keep my walls up high and firm. I was no longer believing the lies that I could not survive without my walls, and that I was alone in the world.

I can now walk in joy, peace, freedom and release as I deal with the circumstances in my life which can still, at times, be quite difficult. I still have to walk through such emotions as pain, anger, frustration, and sadness, but it is different now. I am not stuck there. I walk through it hand in hand with the Lord. I know that He will not leave me nor forsake me. He will not abandon me. He loves me.

I still have many things to take care of but now I ask for His help in everything, and He does not disappoint. Either sending me an unexpected person at the perfect time or giving me the strength to do whatever it is I need to do, He has helped me in amazing ways. Once, when I was having a pity party, my friend said, "Calli, you are not alone. Jesus is with you." My sarcastic reply (Sorry, Lord) was, "Yah, but Jesus doesn't shovel snow!" When I came home that day, and following every snowfall since, my driveway has been cleared!

I am no longer alone. That deep loneliness that had plagued me for so long has been replaced by intimacy with Him that helps me and grows stronger every day. He guides me, walks with me, teaches me, sings over me, laughs with me, and releases His angels to help me. He even gave me a song of our journey together!

I am no longer alone.

Surrendered in Your Arms

Oh Lord, my God, You are my rock,
My tower, and my hope.
Oh Lord, my God, You are my love,
My fortress, and my peace.

Chorus

Hold me, carry me, I stay surrendered in Your arms.
Hold me, carry me, I stay surrendered in Your arms.

Oh Lord, my God, You are my strength,
You are my armor and shield.
Oh Lord my God, You reign in me,
Your Word is healing my soul.

My heart is Yours, my life is Yours,

My pain, my sadness and joy.
I lay it all down, before You Lord,
I lay it all down at Your feet.
I lay it all down, before You Lord,
I lay it all down at Your feet.

I would like to stand with you in prayer. You are not alone.

Dear Heavenly Father,

The glory of the Lord is man fully alive and set free. Let Your presence flow in this place, and be a beautiful, fragrant presence that washes over me and begins to heal all the wounded places of my heart so that I may be fully alive and set free. Lord, I lay my heart down before You, open and vulnerable ... have Your way in my life. Please break the chains that are holding me in bondage. Let the living water of Your Holy Spirit flow; let it be the living truth that heals me from any form of abandonment that is hindering me.

Lord, I pray that Holy Spirit will empower me to take each healing step patiently, waiting on Your perfect time, because You, Lord, do everything right in Your time. Lord, I pray for Holy Spirit to fill me with Your grace and hope. Pour Your patience into me. I thank You that Your Word says You will set the captives free and heal the brokenhearted and I trust that this is for me. I thank You that Your grace is sufficient to help me through all the situations I face and that You will be my strength to work through every detail and every step I face in overcoming abandonment. When I am overwhelmed, help me to trust that You are making changes all the time, even when I cannot see them nor understand them. I thank You, Lord, for the day that I will be totally set free.

Thank You, Lord, that You are a gentle, kind God, and You do not force Your will on me. I thank You that You ask me to submit onto You not to control or abuse me, but to lead me and guide me. I thank You that I do not have to be afraid-- Your plan for me is good. Help me to release unto You, all those areas that I am still hanging onto.

Heavenly Father, I pray against the fear of being alone and of being lonely. Help me realize that loneliness is a state of mind, and an issue of the heart that can be healed. Help me be emotionally and spiritually healthy enough to be full of joy and peace, and fully secure even when I am not in the presence of others. Help me to understand that I am never alone; You are always with me. I pray that You can help me learn to receive my affirmations and feelings of acceptance from You, and You alone. I thank You that it is in the place of being alone with You that I can discover who I am and that You love me. Restore to me my vision of who I am as a person, and my vision of how You see me. When I am afraid of being alone, help me to realize that healing and blessing happen when I am alone with You.

Teach me to express to You all the emotions You have given me to help me find my healing. And Lord, I forgive all those in my life that I feel have abandoned me in some way. By forgiving them, I release them into Your hands, and I release myself to be healed.

Reveal to me any vulnerabilities I still have that leave me open to being abused and abandoned so that I can receive healing, be fully healthy and whole, and so that I can close and seal that door in my life to the enemy for all of my future days.

Right now, Lord, I come against any lies of the enemy or false beliefs that I have held that allowed him any legal rights into my life. Please reveal them to me and show me the truth. (Give Holy Spirit time to reveal any of the lies that need to be broken.)

Lord, if I have believed that "I don't deserve to be loved," " I am unloveable," "No one will choose me," "I will always be alone," " I am worthless if I am alone," "I have to do everything, and fight every battle alone," "It's my fault," "No one else will love me," "People will always leave me," or _____ (name any revealed lies), I pray You break it off me right now, and whisper Your truth into my spirit. Forgive me for partnering with it in any way.

Please take my negative experience of feeling abandoned, and replace it with being fully sold out and committed to You; bought and paid for by the blood of the Lord Jesus Christ, and totally abandoned unto You. Let me know that I am not abandoned, I am not alone, but You are right here by my side, singing over me and dancing with me in all I do. Thank You, Lord, for loving me. I pray this in Jesus' name.

Amen.

*F*or everything there is a season, a time for every activity under heaven. A time to tear and a time to mend.

A time to be quiet and a time to speak.

Ecclesiastes 3:1,7

$\mathcal{F}$or God as said, "I will never fail you. I will never abandon you." So we can say with confidence, "The Lord is my helper, so I will have no fear."

Hebrews 13:5b-6a

$\mathcal{T}$he Spirit of the Sovereign Lord is upon me, for the Lord has anointed me to bring good news to the poor. He has sent me to comfort the brokenhearted and to proclaim that captives will be released and prisoners will be freed. He has sent me to tell those who mourn that the time of the Lord's favor has come, and with it, the day of God's anger against their enemies. To all who mourn in Israel, he will give a crown of beauty for ashes, a joyous blessing instead of mourning, festive praise instead of despair. In their righteousness, they will be like great oaks that the Lord has planted for his own glory.

Isaiah 61:1-3

*T*he LORD says, "I will guide you along the best pathway for your life. I will advise you and watch over you.

Psalm 32:8

*B*end down, O LORD, and hear my prayer; answer me, for I need your help. Protect me, for I am devoted to you. Save me, for I serve you and trust you. You are my God. Be merciful to me, O LORD, for I am calling on you constantly. Give me happiness, O LORD, for I give myself to you. O LORD, you are so good, so ready to forgive, so full of unfailing love for all who ask for your help. Listen closely to my prayer, O LORD; hear my urgent cry. I will call to you whenever I'm in trouble, and you will answer me.

Psalm 86:1-7

*S*o humble yourselves under the mighty power of God, and at the right time he will lift you up in honor.

1Peter 5:6

Dear Child,

Chaos will come to order as you seek Me. My will becomes your own as you seek Me with all your heart. The intimacy for which you seek is attainable by My spirit when you seek Me. You will be overtaken with love and hope. You will know My presence is real; My intimacy is real. I will reveal it to you as you seek Me with all your heart. Keep surrendering, keep being in My presence. I will flood you with hope, with life, with love, with knowledge. I will help others through the heart knowledge you gain by being in My presence. You will teach others to revel in My presence. Yes, your journey has been hard and long, but your struggles, your life has been worth it, as I use it to draw others unto Me. The joy, love and peace you seek are yours as you seek Me. I will be with you. Every step of the way I will be with you. I will guide you. You do not have to figure it out, or strive in your flesh. You do not have to make the plan. I will guide you, step by step. You are Mine and Mine alone. Your heart now belongs to Me, and I will give you all the treasures you seek. The insecurities will fade away, and you will step out confidently. Rest in My presence, rest in My hope, rest in My joy, and I will reveal it to you, step by step. Step by step is your joy. Step by step is your hope. Step by step is your song--your life. I am pouring out on you like the sweet spring rain. I pour My life out on you. I pour My heart out on you. You are okay. You are strong. You are full of hope. Your trust is in Me, and I will pour out My spirit on you. I love you.

♥ Jesus

Under the Grip of Fear

During the journey of my healing, one of the major issues that kept confronting me was fear. I recognized that it had been manifesting in my life in several ways, for many years. One was the exaggerated startle reflex, where I would physically jump, and my heart would practically go into cardiac arrest when someone unexpectedly showed up directly behind or in front of me. Other fear reflexes included not being able to stand in front of an open window at night, jumping at every unexpected sound, especially at night, keeping me from a deep sleep. Many of my decisions were driven by fear especially in regards to parenting or dealing with anything unfamiliar, or going places by myself. I would also constantly go into a mind numbing panic at every confrontation, especially with Rob. Another major way fear reared its nasty face was in the constant sensation that every time I opened a door, or the shower curtain, or went into another room, someone would be standing right there waiting for me with evil intentions. It was stated matter-of-factly in my first ever prophetic word, from a well-known prophet in our region (who knew very little about me and knew nothing about my history).

"I feel like you have been very … it is almost like you have been spooked in a way; it is because of your past experiences, it is like 'What is going to get me now?' It is like you are waiting for something to come out of the closet and scare you. It is like around every corner something bad is going to happen to you, and God wants to put an end to that thought process. I believe that there is a healing that has come for you, Calli, and God is saying that it is time to have a new confidence and to be able to move forward confidently. I think it's time that you rise up and scare the enemy off your life instead of being a victim of what he has brought; fear and intimidation, into your life. I feel like the Lord is telling you to stand on those foundation blocks, and it is time for you to roar back at the enemy…" (December 2009.)

That had been my life. I always knew who was going to get me, I just never knew exactly when, or how, or how much, or what would trigger it. It could be something I said or didn't say, or how I said it. It could be something I did or didn't do; how I looked, or what I overlooked. It could be how I walked, talked, what I thought or didn't realize I was supposed to think. Maybe this time it was what I felt or didn't feel, believed or didn't believe, agreed or disagreed with … The list was endless. Nothing about me was deemed acceptable in Rob's eyes. Nothing I could do or say was right, or enough … it was never enough. Even if I gave "my everything" to "do it right" … it didn't matter. It never mattered. It was never enough in any facet; never good enough, never pleasing enough, never loving enough, never quite right … and that would give him the excuse he needed to unleash with wrath.

I could usually feel the storm building and often I could predict when it would hit. Other times, I had no idea it was about to descend. I could be walking peacefully along, hand in hand with Dr. Jekyll, and suddenly seemingly out of the blue, Mr. Hyde would jump out in full force, and attack; always verbally, sometimes physically. Through many years of this "training," I began to understand that it is often not the present circumstances that would set him off, but something that was previously said (or not said, done or not done …), and for the last few hours, or even days, he would have had an internal dialogue that would build up the circumstances into something that it wasn't. He would supply his beliefs, explanations, and my supposed motives behind it (usually invented and twisted, with not much rationality or evidence to support it). The result was that he had become convinced that I had maliciously and intentionally done something that disrespected or belittled him in some way. At first I was shocked when I discovered how he got from 'A' (what I had originally said or did …) to 'B' (how he interpreted it as a vindictive attack against him). After a while, it no longer mattered. The result was always the same, whether I had some responsibility in it or not. I would bear the brunt of his rage.

In one particular circumstance as we walked peacefully (or so I thought) along the golf course, he calmly told me he was going to "bury me under a golf green." To this day, I do not know what I had said/did/thought/believed/missed doing to receive that first seemingly unprovoked, not so subtle hint that he could kill me at any time. I was in shock after that; my emotions frozen as I let the unreality of my reality settle deep into my soul.

Other comments, such as "I'll throw you off a balcony," or "I'll smash your head through the windshield" (while grabbing my face hard enough to leave a bruise to make his point thoroughly), were not quite as vague and had the same impact of depositing fear into my heart. At one point, something not too serious had happened to my son, which provoked the reaction: "You better be prepared to put a bullet in your head if anything happens to him on your watch. If you don't, I will." Needless to say, these types of threats set up a fear-based lifestyle, not only in parenting but in all my decision making.

Sometimes, these internally escalating conversations led him to roll over onto me in the middle of the night and grab my throat. He would go at me time, and time again, for hours, trying to make me be, think, and feel the exact way he wanted me to be, think and feel. More than once, he kicked me to the foot of the bed--"like a dog where you belong." Other times, he would grab my pajama shirt so roughly that it would rip off several buttons. Then, after having said all manner of horrible things about me, he would force intimacy on me. I believe this was an aggressive act of power to try to force me to submit. At times, I would run away and barricade myself in another room. Other times I would just submit, crying softly to myself, knowing that it would be over sooner this way, as fighting meant the tirade could go on for hours, days, or even weeks. Submission usually brought with it a period of grace as he temporarily got what he wanted. But at what price? What affect did this have on my heart, my soul, and my spirit?

Regrettably, I never reported any of the assaults. Fear kept me boxed in. Reporting it would, I believed, make him mad and I didn't feel that even the police could protect me. He was calm and patient in a warped, vengeful sense, and would eventually find the opportunity to make me pay. He always did. If I left ... would I even then be safe? Or just waiting in fear every day until he found me?

Needless to say, I developed a very "fear based perspective" that remained with me even long after I finally left. There were many, many events, actions, words and gestures over the years that filled me with so much fear I didn't even know where to begin to face it, let alone heal from it. I didn't even remember all that had happened to me in the ten years of marriage, so how could I begin to deal with each instance, or pray them through, as I believed I had to do?

Oh, but God is merciful, and He loves to heal us as we let Him into those dark, wounded places of our heart. Over the years, He brought people into my life that helped me work through each memory as they surfaced. It was almost like slowly unwrapping bandages from wounds upon wounds. Little bit by little bit, more would be exposed, and I would be able to deal with that particular piece. Too much at a time, and I would not have been able to survive the pain of the process. But slowly, I noticed my coping mechanisms for the fear subside. I could go in front of an open window at night. My heart would not go into a frenzy (quite as much) when someone startled me. I no longer had to unplug the phone or go into panic mode after another confrontation with Rob.

Still, I had that sensation that someone would be standing behind every door I opened, just waiting to get me. I had dealt with so many of the things that triggered my fear, but the thought that I would not be free from it until I had healed from every individual episode that had ever traumatized me was overwhelming and seemingly impossible. However, one of my mentors assured me that I did not have to deal with every incident of trauma. God would reveal a key episode, and from there it would be like a domino effect, bringing healing in all the other areas. During the Elijah House trauma course, in the spring of 2015, this was precisely what happened. God revealed to me one specific incident that allowed that particular aspect of fear legal rights into my life:

Rob had somehow found out that I had been keeping a journal, and he wanted me to give it to him. There was no way I was doing that, but I also believed I could no longer keep it. (Which now makes no sense, because I had kept several of my previous journals, and they were still safely hidden!) Panicking, I crept downstairs in the middle of the night to destroy it. While I was ripping up the pages, I looked up to see him standing on the stairs, watching me. It was like something out of a horror movie. I was terrified beyond breath. I did not know what he would do. Miraculously, and for some reason I don't understand, he was satisfied with my actions and just went back upstairs. Even though he had not touched me and did not utter even a word, somehow that was the event that had rooted this fear so tightly around my heart. Once I prayed over that key incident, the fear in me was broken, and Jesus gave me the joy of complete freedom. At times, as new situations occur, I notice it trying to creep back into my life, but I pray against it immediately--or ask for prayer--and it has no choice but to leave.

Through all this, God taught me that sometimes it takes all the fights against the circumstances of life, the injuries inflicted on us, especially by those we love, and the overwhelming fears we face, in order to bring up the deep places of pain that we have buried in the depths of our hearts. We don't want to face them, so we don't. We hide them deep within and pray that they never surface. Nevertheless, God allows those storms that roar and rage so that everything inside us can be churned up and tossed around until it all becomes exposed. As raw and painful as that is, it is the only way these deep places of pain and fear in our hearts can be revealed and healed. Without this revelation, the pain and fear stay trapped in our bodies and souls and torments us. It breeds such things as anxiety, disconnection, discouragement, depression, sadness and discontentment. It hinders the work of Holy Spirit within us and prevents us from walking in the complete joy and freedom God has for us. It stops the flow of peace and trust toward the Father. In times of storms, when the waves rise hard against us and threaten to tear us apart, do not turn inward and try to protect, conceal, or preserve. Instead, spread your arms wide in the very heart of the storm, expose your heart, and tell the Lord: "I am Yours. Forgive me, guide me, teach me; do with me what You will. I am forever Yours."

Being released from fear is a huge part of healing and will bring enormous change into your life. It will bring a whole new level of confidence to the very core of your being. Take the time to pray this prayer through as many times as you need. I know how hard it is, but you can do this, with God's help.

Lord,

I thank You that You are my rock, my strong tower, and my place of refuge when I am afraid. I need You now to heal some deep, deep fears that have had a grip on me. They have been robbing me of life and vitality, and I cannot shake them on my own. Father, I pray You remove and heal any fear that was brought in when I was a child, because I was abused, abandoned, betrayed or neglected by a person in authority. Replace the fear with confidence in You, Lord, and restore my ability to trust. I pray that I can be changed and renewed through Your love for me. I don't have to try change myself. I trust You to do it. Please give me Your truth, and allow me to be set free by Your truth. I know I am Your child--loved, valued, and treasured. Help me to find my identity in You.

Lord, in all those times when I was afraid, I sometimes wonder where You were. Please reveal to me where You were in all those tough places in my life. Help me to always be able to find You when I need You to be my defender. Help me learn to call on Your name in my times of need. Please heal all the trauma I carry in my body and all its effects, because of all the fearful events I have endured in my life. Please release me from the constant dread I carry in my belly, like always expecting bad news, always expecting bad things to happen to me and to those I love, or for something to be waiting around every corner to "get me." Let me be fearless, with my confidence firmly rooted in You. Emblazon the word "fearless" on my heart and in my mind. Give me new thought patterns and new, godly responses to every situation. Transform my mind and heart, physically, mentally and emotionally. I know You have not given me a spirit of fear, but of love, power, and a sound mind. I declare this truth in my life. Wash my mind and my heart clean so that I can live by this truth. I want to rise and scare the enemy off my life, instead of always being scared. I no longer want to be a victim, but I want to stand on the firm foundation blocks You give me, and roar back at the enemy.

Right now, I come against the spirit of fear and intimidation, and I tell you to leave in the name of Jesus. You have no power. I pray that fear and intimidation would no longer control my life in any way. I will no longer allow fear to keep my mouth shut up. I will speak out boldly, in all areas that You lead me, Lord.

I pray that You show me any key incidents that have happened in my life that need to be healed, which will lead to the healing of all other areas. Father, I pray You break down any strongholds of fear that are keeping me bound. Reveal them to me by the power of Holy Spirit. Show me all the things I am believing which are really lies according to Your Word, that are keeping me in captivity. (Give Holy Spirit time to reveal any of these strongholds or lies. Trust that whatever comes to mind that seems to make sense, is a revelation from God.)

....

I pray now, in Jesus' name, that You break off the stronghold of _____ in my life. I break off the lie that _____, in Jesus' name. Fill my heart and mind with Your truth. I break off all power that was given to these strongholds and lies in my life. I will partner with them no longer. I choose to believe Your word that You are my place of safety. Cover me with Your feathers, and shelter me with Your wings. Become more, and more real to me, Lord, as I seek You.

Father God, right now I come against the spirit of suffocation--any act or word that was said or done against me that tried to take my breath away, and any mental, physical and emotional effects it had on me. By the shed blood of Christ, I bind that up right now, and send it to the foot of the cross, to be handed over to Jesus. I ask for complete healing of the trauma in my body, soul and spirit. I pray against all hyper-vigilance in my body and soul, right down to the cellular level, that came in with the traumas that I have experienced.

Please return all my body systems to the exact way You designed them to be. I ask that You remove all nightmares, all pictures in my mind, and any physical manifestations caused by trauma and abuse, and replace them with dreams of godly things, images of You, and a completely healthy body. Send Your love deep down into my heart, Lord. Like a river of healing water, flood through me and bring complete cleansing ... wash out all the fear, shock, trauma, terror and ugliness, Lord, and replace it with the gift of peace of mind and heart.

Help me, Lord, to forgive those people involved in hurting me so that I can walk in freedom, not in bondage. I release them from my hands and put them into Your capable hands. Help me to forgive myself as well, and help me to understand that I did not nor do not deserve any of these bad things that happened to me, even if I contributed to it in some way. Help me to forgive You too, Lord, for the times that I felt that You were not there for me when I needed You. I choose to believe that You were there with me, and You were crying over my pain, even more than I was.

Lord, I pray against any social anxiety and mistrust I might carry because of my past, and I ask You to replace it with many godly friends. Your Word says that the godly will crowd around us, and we can live a long, satisfying life. I want that for my life, Lord. Send me those friends of the heart that I can talk with and pray with, to learn more about You.

Lord, I want to feel again. I have been numb for so long, trying to hide the pain. I want to invite Holy Spirit in to do what needs to be done so I will feel again, and not be scared to do so. I want to be able to walk through the pain in a healthy way so that I can finally heal from it and be held captive no longer. I need the power of Holy Spirit to be finally free. I cannot do it on my own. I ask for healthy feelings and healthy emotional responses in all areas. Take away any irrational fears or phobias, and any addictions and unhealthy coping mechanisms that I have used to try get by in life. I no longer want them, nor any people to control and manipulate my life, but ask You Lord, to take over.

Help me to release all the mental torment that results from trying to understand the things that will never make sense, and from trying to figure out all the things that are impossible for me to figure out. Help me just to turn them over to You, and accept that You will take care of all that needs to be done. Please tear down any fear based perspectives that manifest themselves by affecting my decisions about my future, my parenting, new opportunities, people, or in any other areas of my life. I want a new beginning. I want to be a new creation, one that walks in complete freedom. Your Word says, "Whoever the Son sets free, is free indeed," and I claim this. I will hide from life no longer! I pray this in the mighty name of Jesus.

Amen.

*C*ommit everything you do to the LORD. Trust him, and he will help you. He will make your innocence radiate like the dawn, and the justice of your cause will shine like the noonday sun.

Psalm 37:5-6

*P*raise the LORD, who is my rock. He trains my hands for war and gives my fingers skill for battle. He is my loving ally and my fortress, my tower of safety my rescuer. He is my shield, and I take refuge in him.

Psalm 144:1-2

*A*nd you will know the truth, and the truth will set you free. So if the Son set you free, you are truly free.

John 8:32, 36

*F*or God has not given us a spirit of fear and timidity,

but of power, love, and self-discipline.

2 Timothy 1:7

"*I* am leaving you with a gift--peace of mind and heart.

And the peace I give is a gift the world cannot give.

So don't be troubled or afraid.

John 14:27

*T*hose who live in the shelter of the Most High will find

rest in the shadow of the Almighty. This I declare

about the LORD: He alone is my refuge, my place of

safety; he is my God, and I trust Him. For he will rescue

you from every trap and protect you from deadly disease.

He will cover you with his feathers. He will shelter you

with his wings. His faithful promises are your armor and

protection.

Psalm 91:1-4

*S*uch people will not be overcome by evil. Those who are righteous will be long remembered. They do not fear bad news; they confidently trust the LORD to care for them. They are confident and fearless and can face their foes triumphantly.

Psalm 112:6-8

I look up to the mountains – does my help come from there? My help comes from the LORD, who made heaven and earth! He will not let you stumble; the one who watches over you will not slumber. Indeed, he who watches over Israel never slumbers or sleeps. The LORD himself watches over you! The LORD stands beside you as your protective shade. The sun will not harm you by day, nor the moon at night. The LORD keeps you from all harm and watches over your life. The LORD keeps watch over you as you come and go, both now and forever.

Psalm 121:1-8

Dear Child,

My peace I give you. Fear does not come from Me. My plans for you are good. Do not give in to your fear. Give it over to Me in every circumstance. Walk in confidence as you walk with Me. My love is perfect, casting out all fear. My patience is constant and enduring. Walk with Me as always. I will lead you. Talk with Me as always. I will guide you. I will be your strength, your armor, your shield. Make Me your rock. Make Me your fortress. I am your strong tower that will protect you, not only in words but in real might and in real battle. Keep releasing any fear as it crops up and pray over it. Draw on My strength. Draw on My love, My security. Yes, they are more than words. This goes so much deeper than words. Words are the catalyst to the true meanings of the heart, but only the catalyst. There is so much more. Think of a tree, with the roots going deep down into the soil, to unknown places. People only see what they see in the tree, that which is above the ground. But the depth of the tree, the heart and soul of the tree, are the roots that tap into the earth, the underground spring of water that it needs. Be the roots. Be the depth that the people cannot see. Reach down and access My healing water.

♥ Jesus

Overcoming Rejection

Realization hit me as I struggled to cut up some peppers and make sandwiches at my friend's house. I was hesitant because I was afraid I would do it wrong. And this was two years after I had been on my own again! Where had my confidence gone?

I have always considered myself fairly normal in most aspects of life. I have been a fairly high achiever academically, winning the odd scholarship and award here and there, and most people label me as quite capable and competent. I can get a lot of work done in a short amount of time, and I can handle many things at once. I have always excelled at most sports that I have tried, except golf and water skiing, though I am far from Olympic material. I have completed several mini triathlons but have never attempted a full one. I have exercised off and on throughout most of my life. I love anything outdoors, but am not a diehard mountain climber or anything like that. Most often, I prefer a tent and bonfire to a night in a hotel--but I'll take that too when I get the chance.

My body type is average. I consider myself "Pretty on a good day," but I am not photogenic. I am artistic and creative; good, but not over the top gifted. I love gardening but have successfully killed every indoor plant that I've ever had, often in creative ways. My friends know that, while on some days they'll walk into my home and find it neat and tidy, other days they won't be able to find the kitchen counter. Usually, there is one room or closet that desperately cries for a little more attention. I am not perfect. I will never be perfect, nor have I ever claimed to be perfect. I am, however, quite normal.

My children are highly gifted musically. They get this from both sides of the family ... but not from me. I can do a great impression of the "Elaine dance" from the old Seinfeld series, and I can dance and jump before the Lord, but I am not exactly what one would consider graceful. I am an introvert. I am shy and quiet in a crowd and do not stand out. I was successful in public speaking in my profession for many years. In large groups, I am quiet but can hold my own in small groups or one-on-one. People who did not know me well used to tease my friends, asking "What do you do with Calli when you are out for coffee?" They would laugh and assure them that I did have much to say. I am a good, loyal friend. I am more of a self-described sidekick than the one out in front and center, and I am okay with that. It is part of who I am.

I have excelled professionally in my classroom and have several achievements at the provincial and national levels. I have currently fifteen professional publications in the field of language education, with three different companies. I have worked hard all my life to achieve what I felt called to do ... and yet I went through a period where I could not confidently make a sandwich for someone else. I had been dismantled, piece by piece, for many years.

When I began dating Rob, he seemed genuinely interested in me and in what I had to say and generally, in what I was all about. It was nice. Most of my previous interactions with boys, and then men, were more one-sided. Either I was taken with them, and they were not interested, or vice-versa. Or, there was a mutual interest but after a while, it didn't seem to go anywhere beyond that. Finally, with Rob, it seemed that the feelings were equally mutual and fairly strong.

Flash forward to a short time later. I walked in the front door to the question: "How was your day?" only to have my answer interrupted with "I don't want a novel." I was stunned. Had his interest been feigned, and now the marriage license canceled the need to impress? Or was he changing, uninterested already in his new bride? It did not matter. The result was the same. His choice of the newspaper over me, even when I was going to be leaving for several days, and snapping on the radio for the one and a half hour drive, though I desperately tried to talk to him, became the norm. My greeting after a weekend away was not the imagined "Hi honey, how was your weekend?" but rather, "How the hell am I supposed to fit all your crap in my car?"

I began to feel a little less than loved; not exactly cherished! I was finding we were very different; gone were the fun things we had done before we were married. Struggling to at least spend some time together, and not be ignored all the time, I would suggest we build on our commonalities. I was shut down again with "Are you thick and dense? You just don't get it. I have to spend all my time on work."

My work, on the other hand, seemed to diminish in importance. Once upon a time he seemed to like that I was a teacher. His mom was a teacher. My dad was a teacher. He had supported my sideline of publishing and selling teacher resources. He even proudly sat in on one of the workshops I gave at a conference. Of course, the truth in that too was soon revealed. It became "You are just a teacher." "It's not brain surgery." "Those who can't do, teach," and "They set the bar of expectations for teachers so low." He became especially derogatory of some of the areas in which I taught, belittling and mocking them in front of our children.

More, and more I felt devalued as his general comments grew harder and became more frequent. I constantly heard such words as: "I have a lifetime of good memories with Dan (a friend who died) … with you I have nothing. You are blowing it." "I only married you to get the house. That was my plan all along." "I don't see you in my vision. You don't have any plans or goals." "I know who I want to be with, and it's not you." "You are just someone I f***."

"You have no taste." "You have no fashion sense." "Everything you know is white bread." "You can't carry on a conversation." "You can't catch on to basic concepts that a two-year-old can understand." "I only married you because I was banking on you changing." "You underwhelm me."

You get the idea. My new names mimicked a disgusting list from a Dr. Phil episode: "fat a**, stupid, a pet, lower than a dog at my heels, b****, half-breed Gypsy s***, idiot, crazy, slob, lazy, smart a**, tramp, slut, whore, a few more I won't write, and, of course, the c-word, in various vulgar combinations.

Then came the criticism about how I looked. This flew at me hard and mean like I had never experienced before. Though I was of an average build and had been since we met, my weight became a main focus. "I can't love you unless you have a nice a**." Pardon me? I always thought love went much deeper than that.

"I see myself with someone slim and attractive," was one of his more subtle putdowns. Soon, it was that I wore my makeup like a clown. He didn't like the way I wore my hair. He didn't like the way I dressed. When I looked around at how other women were dressing, I was, as always, nicely in the middle. I did not wear sexy lingerie around the house, nor high heels when grocery shopping as he wanted, but I was not sloppy nor unkempt by any standards. I did once make the mistake of showing up in front of him and his dad in a pair of sweatpants as I was on my way to the gym, but I never made that mistake again! Nor do I, to this day, wear sneakers unless I am doing something physical. I had been thoroughly conditioned. But, it was never quite good enough. Taking extra time and care to get some approval, I was met with "You should be wearing a push-up bra," or "You need polish on your shoes." I could never win. Some days, as was typical of our bizarre reality, I was the most beautiful girl he could imagine ...

But most days, he didn't like the way I talked, walked, carried myself, ate, or that I wasn't the life of the party, turning heads with my dynamic personality as soon as I entered a room. He wanted a trophy wife, and I just wasn't cutting it. It was hard to take. Since I didn't go into the marriage as a trophy wife, how and why would he expect me to all of a sudden become one?

I felt the most degraded when he attacked me as a woman. Part of his issue was that I loved to play team sports, though it cost me dearly at an emotional level. He wanted me to be fit, but he wanted me only to participate in the individual sports of which he approved. My triathlon training was fine. He totally supported me cycling and even bought me a fantastic bike. Weightlifting was encouraged, and he even attempted to make me into a powerlifter, like him. However, team sports were forbidden. Messages about games would be deleted from the phone and it would be a fight every time I left the house for a game--both before and after having children. Rude comments were made. I began to understand that he saw me as less feminine because I played soccer and basketball. He associated these sports with sexuality. Soccer and basketball players were lesbians, he believed, so he began to refer to me as butch, dike, lesbo, and lesbian.

The other big issue was S – E – X. Often I would retaliate to some of his demeaning remarks with comebacks such as, "My friends like me! They think I'm okay!" He stuck the metaphoric knife in my back with "Yeah, but they don't have to live with you." I had nothing with which to defend myself. During the times of sanity, he was very satisfied with me as a wife. When he was mean, he cut to the very core of my being. On those days, if I wore the wrong thing to bed or did something else wrong, the attacks would be ferocious:

~ You make me puke! I don't get anything from you as a woman--or as a wife.

~ You are blowing it. I will get sex somewhere else. I would rather sleep with a goat.

~ We have nothing. You are a male in drag. Be a female. You turn me off so much. I can't get it back.

~ I want romance and mystery.

I could not be the sex kitten that he wanted, forever trying to seduce him in every manner possible. When I tried, I felt so phony that I could not stand it. So, the attacks continued and would last nearly too long to bear. If he ran out of insults in the moment yet didn't feel as though he had quite completed his attack, he would wake me up in a few hours (if I dared to fall asleep), and go at me again. Sometimes a physical or sexual assault would follow.

Before I had kids, I would often leave at some point, or lock myself in another room. However after kids, I would not leave without them, and I had no place left to hide. The living room couch felt too vulnerable, as he could be standing over me without my knowing it. At least by staying in the same bed I would be woken up by any movements he made. Somehow, it felt safer this way yet at the same time, it made me feel altogether hopeless. I felt like I was leaving myself open to being easy prey, not even able to protect myself anymore--like I no longer mattered, even to myself.

It was not pretty. I was not loved, honored or cherished. I hated it. I hated him. I hated myself. I felt like I was going to explode. I wanted to cut my wrists. Not in a suicidal way, but rather to feel some release from the blackness that was overtaking me from the inside. I remember sketching myself blindfolded in a coffin, with black scribbles all around the outside. It was a representation of what was happening to me on the inside. (See Appendix 3.)

On the outside, people were noticing the effects as well, as I slowly began to disintegrate. My sister's friends would ask what was wrong with me after I was unable to make eye contact when meeting them, nor carry on much of a conversation. It was becoming a self-fulfilling prophecy. Friends of friends, and friends of my own began to describe me to others as "a stick ... a shell ... a dish rag." I even began lashing out at sales clerks and basketball opponents at the slightest perceived incompetence or provocation. This was not me; never had been me. Even after I was out of the relationship for two years, my current employer had to go to several people who knew me well, to ensure that I could handle the job he wanted to offer me.

My resumé was extensive and strong, but he saw me fall apart in church time, and time again, and wondered if I was still capable.

My professional abilities had never been in question before. I had always managed to hold at least that part of my life together.

I spent so many years being ground down into nothing … having every fiber of my being shredded beyond recognition. Sometimes I felt like I had nothing left. Some days I did not have anything left. I was one of the broken ones. Sometimes I am amazed that I survived mentally and emotionally at all, and I didn't end up in a psychiatric ward, counting tiles to avoid reality. I am so thankful I got out when I did. I don't think I would have survived as 'me' much longer. As it was, it was a long, hard road to come back. Nevertheless, I did come back and have even surpassed any place I have ever been. I know it was only by God's grace, and the firm foundation laid by my parents that I did survive to tell my story.

In my healing journey, I have found that the two keys to overcoming rejection are understanding the real measure of truth, and understanding the truth of how God sees me. I had to come to the realization that I was not who Rob said I was, nor was I the way he perceived me to be. The problem was that the whole question of truth had become clouded and distorted in my mind. There is great confusion in our world over the reality of truth. It works something like this: If Rob and I both saw a car drive by and I said, "That is a nice white car," his comment would be, "No, it is black." "No, I saw it, it was white," I would say. He then would come at me so adamantly, trying to convince me that it was black, that I would begin to question myself, thinking that maybe something had distorted my view, a shadow perhaps, or maybe I was simply mistaken. He would come at me again with such conviction: "No, beyond all doubt, it was black … is there something the matter with you or …?"

You now seriously begin to question what you saw, since he so fiercely believed he was right. And with nothing to go back to, to prove it one way or another, you waver and maybe even say, "Yes, maybe you are right (whether you truly believe it or not, but you can no longer be one hundred percent sure, so you no longer want to argue, and even if you are one hundred percent sure, the argument would continue all night, so you give in …) maybe it was black…"

"What are you CRAZY? That car was white!" (Let the manipulation and crazy-making games begin!)

Though this is a fictitious example to help bring some understanding, this sort of thing unfolds over and over in many different forms in abusive relationships and begins to distort reality. You may even begin to base truth only on what comes out of his mouth. In talking to people in abusive situations, you'll notice we often begin with "But he said …"

I only received the revelation of this way of thinking several months after I had left. There was an incident with our boy. Rob phoned and told me himself what had happened with our son. I assume it was so he could give his account before I talked to our son. Later, Rob came to my house, and we discussed it again in the driveway. That night, my son told me what happened. He soon brought it up again, referring to it as "The Great Smack-down."

Much later, maybe a month or two, when I brought it up again in reference to what a counselor (one of our seven) had said was eventually going to happen, Rob got right in my face. His finger pointed inches from me, his eyes flashed fire, and he boldly stated: "That did not happen! That is a lie!"

BOOM! The shock of the revelation was like getting hit with a two-by-four; I almost saw stars. I knew, beyond the shadow of a doubt, that it had happened ... there was not one question in my mind that it was real or did not happen exactly as he had previously admitted twice, and how my son had described it twice. He was the crazy one!

So many things clicked into place that day. I came to a deep understanding at that moment about dealing with him. To this day, I don't know if he was in such denial that he did not believe he did it, if he was trying to convince himself it did not happen, or if he knew well that it had happened, but there was just no way he was going to admit it or be accountable for it. Nevertheless, IT DID NOT MATTER! The fact was that he was an outright liar. His version of the truth was anything in which he would benefit. Reality had no bearing whatsoever on what came out of his mouth. I could not rely on what he said. Therefore, my truth was no longer based on what he said, EVER. I could not deal rationally with someone irrational. I could not make sense out of nonsense.

I could not combat a situation with common sense, truth, and logic when dealing with a person who was not bound by common sense, truth or logic, but rather driven by saying and doing exactly what suited him in that specific moment to get whatever it was that he wanted. I did not break it, so I could not fix it! In that moment of true realization, it was like time stopped and everything around me paused for several moments as hundreds of calculations and past events flooded my brain. The realization came with stunning force ... I got it! I was NOT who Rob had said I was. I was far from it; usually the polar opposite. His definition of me, his whole perception of me was not reality but merely convenience and manipulation. I finally gained truth… and my strength to stand up to him, to stand up for the truth, the real truth of who I was, was revolutionized in an instant.

As a Christian, after being so deeply rejected, I also needed to relearn and go deeper into my identity in Christ. (See Recommitment/ Salvation prayer in Strategic Survival.) I needed to learn to see myself as God saw me so I could live as God wanted me to live. According to scripture, this is my identity in Christ. This is your identity too, once you put your life in the hands of Christ.

Prayerfully read through the following list and choose a few Scriptures that jump off the page at you. Ask God every day to write that truth of who you are, on your heart. Let it soak deeply into your soul and your spirit. Let it heal your rejection wounds and bring you into a deeper understanding of your identity in Christ, and who God is for you. Ask the Holy Spirit to teach you how to walk it out in your life.

Ephesians 1:6	I am accepted.
Ephesians 2:6	I am seated with Christ in the heavenly realm.
Ephesians 2:10	I am God's masterpiece, created anew in Christ Jesus so I can do the good things He planned for me long ago.
Ephesians 2:18	I have direct access to God through Holy Spirit.
Ephesians 3:12	I am able to approach God with freedom and confidence.
Ephesians 1:4	I am holy and without blame before Him in love.
Deuteronomy 28:13	I am the head and not the tail; I am above only and not beneath.
Ephesians 1:7	I am forgiven of all my sins and washed in the blood.
James 1:22, 25	I am a doer of the Word and blessed in my actions.
Galatians 2:20	It is not I who live, but Christ lives in me.
Hebrews 4:16	I can find grace and mercy in time of need.
Hebrews 13:5	I can always know the presence of God because He never leaves me.
Ephesians 1:3-8	I have been chosen by God and adopted as His child.
Isaiah 54:14	I am far from oppression, and fear does not come near me.
John 1:12	I am a child of God.

Colossians 2:10	I am complete in Jesus Christ.
Colossians 1:11	I am strengthened with all might according to His glorious power.
Colossians 1:14	I am redeemed and forgiven.
Colossians 2:7	I am firmly rooted, built up, established in my faith and overflowing with gratitude.
Colossians 3:3	I am hidden with Christ in God.
Colossians 3:12	I am chosen of God, holy and dearly loved.
1 Corinthians 2:16	I have the mind of Christ.
1 Corinthians 6:17	I am united with God and one spirit with Him.
1 Corinthians 6:19	I am a temple of God. His Spirit and His life lives in me.
1 Corinthians 6:20	I have been bought with a price. I belong to God.
1 Corinthians 12:27	I am a member of Christ's body.
2 Corinthians 1:21	I am established, anointed, and sealed by God.
2 Corinthians 5:17	I am a new creation because I am in Christ.
2 Corinthians 5:18	I am a minister of reconciliation for God.
2 Corinthians 5:20	I am an ambassador for Christ.
2 Corinthians 5:21	I am the righteousness of God in Jesus Christ.
Galatians 3:13	I am redeemed from the curse of sin, sickness, and poverty.
Ephesians 1:1	I am a saint.

1 John 3:3	I am loved.
James 1:5	I can ask God for wisdom and He will give me what I need.
John 15:15	As a disciple, I am a friend of Jesus Christ.
John 15:5	I am a branch of Jesus Christ, the true vine, and a channel of His life.
John 15:16	I have been chosen and appointed to bear fruit.
1 John 4:4	I have the Greater One living in me; greater is He who is in me than he who is in the world.
1 John 5:18	I am born of God, and the evil one cannot touch me.
Matthew 5:14	I am the light of the world.
1 Peter 2:5	I am one of God's living stones, being built up in Christ as a spiritual house.
1 Peter 2:9	I am a part of a chosen generation, a royal priesthood, a holy nation, a purchased people. I show forth the praises of God Who has called me out of darkness and into His marvelous light.
2 Peter 1:3	God has given me all I need to live a godly life.
2 Peter 1:4	I have been given exceedingly great and precious promises by God.
Philippians 3:20	I am a citizen of heaven.

Romans 5:1	I have been justified.
Philippians 4:7	I have the peace of God that passes all understanding.
Philippians 4:13	I can do all things through Christ Who strengthens me.
Philippians 4: 19	God takes care of me and will supply all my needs from his glorious riches.
Philippians 1:6	I am confident that God will complete the good work He started in me.
Philippians 2:13	God works in me to help me do the things He wants me to do.
Psalm 66:8	I am called of God to be the voice of His praise.
Psalm 139:13	You made all the delicate, inner parts of my body and knit me together in my mother's womb.
Psalm 139:14	I praise You, for I am fearfully and wonderfully made.
Psalm 139:16	God saw me before I was born. Every day of my life was recorded in God's book. Every moment was laid out before a single day had passed.
Psalm 139:17	God's thoughts about me are precious.
Revelation 12:11	I am an overcomer by the blood of the Lamb and the word of my testimony.
Isaiah 53:5	I am healed by the stripes of Jesus.

Romans 8:1-2	I am free forever from condemnation.
Romans 5:17	I have received the gift of righteousness and reign as a king in life by Jesus Christ.
Romans 8:37	I am more than a conqueror through Him Who loves me.
Romans 8:28	I am assured that God works for my good in all circumstances.
Romans 8:31-39	I am free from any condemnation brought against me and I cannot be separated from the love of God.
Romans 8:17	I am a joint heir with Jesus, sharing His inheritance with Him.
Romans 8:37	I am more than a conqueror through Him Who loves me.
Timothy 1:7	I have not been given a spirit of fear, but of power, love, and a sound mind.
James 4:7	I am submitted to God, and the devil flees from me because I resist him in the Name of Jesus.
Philippians 3:14	I press on toward the goal to win the prize to which God in Christ Jesus is calling me upward.

For me, the scripture was Ephesians 2:10. *"For we are God's masterpiece. He has created us anew in Christ Jesus, so we can do the good things He planned for us long ago."* I wrote it on my mirror. It's still there. It is becoming more real and more relevant in my life every day as I continue to walk in it.

As I look back over my life--all I have been through, all that I have learned, the depth of intimacy with the Lord I have gained, and the truths that have been deeply etched on my heart--have all brought about changes in me that I could not possibly have developed without my many struggles. I have learned that sometimes God allows you to take the long way around in things ... a journey instead of a short-cut. He wants you to go hard after whatever it is you need. If you take a quick stroll around the block, (as in getting healed, or problems being resolved quickly) there is nothing to prepare for and there is not much new to learn, not much to remember, all soon forgotten.

However, in the journey--the long way around to get to where you need to go and who you need to be--you must plan ahead. You must prepare physically, mentally, and emotionally, put things in place, get things in order, and be intentional. You must dig deep, knowing what may be in store on the road ahead. As you walk along the winding road with your heavy packs weighing you down, meeting circumstances that threaten your very life, stumbling but always getting up, or having someone come alongside and pick you up ... you must rise spiritually to survive. Oh, the things you will learn ... the revelations ... the drastic, deep down astounding changes it will make in your life ... a new way of walking, of talking, of living, a whole new level of trusting ... not soon to be forgotten. Learn who you are, as you take your journey, and as you pray to the Father for His help along the way.

Dear Jesus,

You know all about rejection. You understand what it is not to be accepted to the point of physical violence against Your body, right unto death. Lord Jesus, You know rejection so intimately, even from family and friends, that You are the only person who can come and fill me with the acceptance and honor I need. That is what You died for. Only You can heal those wounds in me, and I thank You that You have experienced that so I can be free. Since You have experienced it, You know every feeling of a rejected person.

You know what it is like to be alone in your darkest hour when you so desire to have someone there with you. Jesus, You know what it is like to be falsely accused, lied about, called names, criticized, spit on, hit and threatened. You were the Lamb sent to the slaughter, but You accept me again and put me in a place of honor because of that very death on the cross. You honored me when You died for me, and that is all the honor I need.

Lord, please help me to expose the secrecy and hiddenness of my rejection so it can be brought into the light so that healing can come. Please lift me up out of the miry clay and set my feet on the solid rock, being Jesus. Lord, I thank You that You spent Your whole ministry honoring women who have been abused and rejected, like the woman at the well who was looking for love. She was rejected by five or six men. Then You came along and loved her, accepted her, honored her, and showed her the way. Lord, I know that You have the opposite attitude to that of my abuser, who said I was not doing enough, not working hard enough, never doing enough of anything. You instead, honor those who just wanted to sit at Your feet, like Mary.

You are Christ the Messiah, the One who lifts up and says "these are women who are after My heart," and that is enough. Thank You for honoring me and lifting me up as I sit at Your feet. Lord, You even honored the prostitute who was crying at Your feet and wiping her tears with her hair. Lord, You were not rejecting of her, but You accepted her and saw her tears of repentance as honor that the other people did not give You by washing Your feet when You came into the room. You lifted her up in front of those men and said she had honored You. I too, Lord, repent of my ways, and sit at Your feet. I thank You that You will be accepting of me, too, and that fills me with peace. Lord, like the good Samaritan, when I have been stripped naked with words and with actions, beaten, abused, and degraded, You come and clothe me with robes of righteousness, bind my wounds, put oil on me, and treat me like royalty. Thank You for doing that for me.

I thank You that even when You were on the cross, You made sure that someone was going to take care of Your mother. Lord, You care deeply for women. You care that I am cared for. Lord, I thank You that in the midst of my rejection, Your heart weeps, and Your heart cries out "Come to me. There is a place in My arms for you, just the way you are. Come to Me, all you who are weary and heavy-laden and I will give you rest." Thank You, Lord, for taking care of me.

Lord Jesus, You not only accepted and honored these women, but You purposefully sought them out. You knew where these women were going to be, and You knew they needed You, so You were there specifically for them. It was no coincidence. In the same way, Lord, the rejected, downtrodden part of me needs You, and I thank You that You are seeking me out, calling me by name, because You want to meet with me. You already know the details of my life, and You seek me out not to judge, but to heal. You see my wounds, and You know I do not always have the strength within me to look for help, or look for You. So I thank You that I have been sought out and searched for by You, Lord. That is truly an honor.

Father God, you knit me together in my mother's womb. Every individual part of me You planned. You know me. Your Word says that I am fearfully and wonderfully made, and You love me. I am the work of Your hands, and You cherish and love the work of Your hands. I thank You, God, that just like clay in the hands of a potter, or paint on the brush of an artist, You carefully plan who I am, what You put into me, and who I will become. You made me totally different from everyone else, because You are a creator, and You love who You create. You have given me a sanctity of life because it was Your hand that has formed me. I am Your creation. I am special to You. I am unique and loved by You. And what You love, no man can degrade. You have put Your Spirit within me, and because You are in me, I am to be cherished, loved, honored and respected. Lord, Your Word says that You have called me by name, and I am Yours. You will be with me. I am precious, honored and loved. By the power of Holy Spirit, I choose to believe Your Word and live by it.

So Lord, by the power of the name of Jesus Christ, I break off the spirit of rejection, and send it to the foot of the cross, to be overcome by the finished work of the shed blood. I will live under it no longer. I break off every curse word thrown at me, and every cruel word and action done to me that was meant to reject or harm me in any way, and any negative thing that was said about who I am or what I am about.

Every curse is broken, in Jesus' name. I thank You, God, that Your Word is powerful and effective and sharper than any double-edged sword. It cuts off the curses. It cuts off everything between soul and spirit that is not of You, Lord. I thank You that the blood of Jesus is over me and that You call me Your bride, Your pure one. Thank You, Lord, for setting me free. You are my mirror. You tell me who I am, and that is deeper and truer than anything else.

I am accepted and honored by You, and that is all that matters--an audience of one. I can now walk out the destiny You have called me to in confidence and grace. I pray this all in Jesus' name.

Amen.

Have a prayer partner read this over you, adapting it as needed, or record it and play it over yourself. Soak it in. God wants to honor you.

I pray honor on you who have born children, who have born the physical brunt of bearing a child. I honor you for just that act. I honor you for being a good mom and for caring for and supporting your children, and loving and accepting them in the midst of being totally rejected yourself. I honor you as a woman who had to live in the secrecy and hiddenness of rejection, but could not tell; could not say anything because of fear. I honor you for your bravery of living through what you had to live through, and still being strong enough to face your pain so that you can heal, and bring healing to your family. I honor you for reaching out for help and being vulnerable, even though it hurts so badly. I honor you that you seek the Lord and want to find His heart, even though your own heart is so broken. I honor you for fighting so hard to try to make it right, and do the right thing. I honor you for giving your all to try to make the best life possible for you and those around you. I honor you for still going on, even though you are weary and weak, and not sure how you are going to make it. I honor you for crying the tears that allow healing to come. I honor you for wanting to feel again, even though not doing so would be so much easier. I honor you for still touching the hearts and lives of others even when your own life was so hard to bear. I honor you for trying to keep your heart soft before God when it would have been easier to shut it down. I honor you for looking so hard for answers when often times there were none. I honor you for protecting your kids in every way you knew how. I honor you for standing up for yourself amidst constant put downs. I honor you for building others up while you were being constantly torn down. I honor you that you valued the sanctity of life that God gave you. Go, in peace, and know that God is with you and that He cares for you incredibly.

So do not throw away this confident trust in the LORD. Remember the great reward it brings you. Patient endurance is what you need now, so that you will continue to do God's will. Then you will receive all that he has promised.

Hebrews 10:35 – 36

*T*hen Jesus said, "Come to me, all you who are weary and carry heavy burdens, and I will give you rest.

Matthew 11:28

But now, O Jacob, listen to the Lord who created you. O Israel, the one who formed you says, "Do not be afraid, for I have ransomed you. I have called you by name; you are mine. When you go through deep waters, I will be with you. When you go through rivers of difficulty, you will not drown. When you walk through the fire of oppression, you will not be burned up; the flames will not consume you.

For I am the LORD, your God, the Holy One of Israel, your Savior. I gave Egypt as a ransom for your freedom; I gave Ethiopia and Seba in your place. Others were given in exchange for you. I traded their lives for yours because you are precious to me. You are honored, and I love you.

"Do not be afraid, for I am with you...

Isaiah 43:1-5

You made all the delicate inner parts of my body, and knit me together in my mother's womb. Thank you for making me so wonderfully complex! Your workmanship is marvelous – how well I know it. You watched me as I was being formed in utter seclusion, as I was woven together in the dark of the womb. You saw me before I was born.

Every day of my life was recorded in your book. Every moment was laid out before a single day had passed. How precious are your thoughts about me, O God. They cannot be numbered! I can't even count them; they outnumber the grains of sand! And when I wake up, you are still with me!

Psalm 139:13-18

Dear brothers and sisters, when troubles come your way, consider it an opportunity for great joy. For you know that when your faith is tested, your endurance has a chance to grow.

James 1:2-4

Dear Child,

You are important. You matter … to Me. That is all that matters … that you matter to Me. I am Your provider, nurturer, husband, lover, counselor, and giver of all joy, peace and life. It is enough in Me. I am all things to you, and will be all things for you if you will just let Me. I stand before you with My hand extended, reaching out in love for you. All you have to do is reach out and grasp My hand. Hold on to Me with both hands, letting go of all things that are hindering you, letting go of all things hurting you. I am here for you. I am your stable foundation, the rock of your salvation, of your life, of your hope. Let go and trust Me with all, and I will not fail. My love never fails. Trust in ME. Look into My eyes, see Me, know Me, find Me. Seek Me. Revel in Me as I revel in you, with you, as we seek together the glorious riches and treasures My Father has laid out for us. You will see. Life with Me is an amazing, adventurous journey, never boring, never lonely, never hurting. The peace--in the storm and the chaos-- covers all. My peace surrounds you like a shield. It covers all, all you give to Me.

♥ Jesus

Under Control

Sometimes we do not realize how easy it is to fall under the control of another person, intentionally, or otherwise. For example, the exploding temper tantrum of a two-year-old when taking something away from them, may make us slightly hesitant the next time that situation occurs, even when we know it is best for them. Constantly dealing with a rebellious student sometimes causes the teacher not to expect quite as much from them as each restriction or request may bring with it an abrasive, time and energy draining battle. Now, imagine similar tantrums in the body of a strong adult male who has thoroughly conditioned you to know how bad it can get, and has often left you wondering if this time, it will be worse.

I heard an analogy recently that explains it well. Picture a family at supper. The daughter casually reminds the father that it is his turn to do the dishes. Getting up and screaming at her about the injustice of this and flipping a chair for effect, he stomps out of the room and slams the door. So … who is the one that will remind him the next time? He has successfully conditioned his family so that he gets what he wants when he wants it. Even if there is never any physical abuse, the unending verbal assaults or the threat of physical violence (which is considered physical abuse) are enough to put tears in your soul, and alter your words, decisions, and actions. You have thus fallen under his control.

For me, it began with little things. I was to make the choice of the restaurant today ... yet somehow we would end up at the one place I specifically requested not to go. I was to choose the marble for the fireplace and the bathroom. Choosing it in several minutes from the options I was given, Rob didn't agree. Three weeks later, with much deliberation (with himself), he came up with the perfect choices--the exact ones I had made previously; but "No, those weren't the ones you chose ..." More reinforcement that what I said didn't matter. I was not allowed a choice nor an opinion.

It was the same with building our house, the one that led to so many problems. Rob and I had looked at only two houses before he refused to look any further. I could agree to build a big home in the small bedroom community, or we would live in an apartment in the city. There was no further discussion, no other options, no compromise.

Even simple things like supper became a tool for control. I was required to have supper in the oven by the time he came home. Sounds simple ... but he refused to let me know when he was on his way ... and it could be anywhere from 5:00 – 10:00 p.m. There was hell to pay when I guessed wrong. He now successfully controlled most of my time after work and well into the evening. Furthermore, I had to get up every morning to make his breakfast and pack his lunch, whether I was working full time or up half the night with a crying baby. Upon my refusal one morning, as I claimed exhaustion, he exerted his power by roughly dragging me out of bed and out of the room by my arm. I got up off the floor and did what he demanded, knowing that it was not something worth fighting for.

I did grow to love our house, and he knew it … so that too became a weapon of choice. When I wasn't a good girl, I would come home to a "For Sale" sign, or to the threat that we would have to sell the house … only to be turned around the next day and be chastised that I was going to cause us to lose the house.

After unleashing his rant, whatever the situation of the moment, he followed up with "I have said what I need to say, now I will wait for it to be done. There is no compromise," or "I will continue to do that to you until you get the message." I usually got the message quickly. Some things I continued to fight against, but many things I had to eventually let go of. It was too much for me to carry. Far too heavy for the little strength I had left.

Control sometimes came in the form of greatly twisting, distorting or exaggerating truths in front of others. My occasional glass of wine became "drinking too much" to my mom. My sister-in-law was dutifully informed that I was "out partying with a married man and a single man." He neglected to add that I was at a teammate's home for our soccer windup, with my entire women's team and a couple of their significant others. He had been invited, but as usual, had declined.

Credit cards were taken, bank statements monitored, the internet and cable cut and insurance policies threatened to be canceled, all in attempts to either punish me, teach me a lesson, or control my actions. Guilt became another form of control. Rob made things extremely difficult for me, then turned it back on me because I was not "willing to be in the trenches with him when things got tough." I think we had different theories of that idea. "Kids from divorced families have the highest suicide rates. Are you willing to wear that one?" was a deep cutting guilt tactic, one that was hard to bear. However, I knew it was not any safer nor healthier to live as we were living.

Things were constantly escalating. The more I gave in to his demands, the more demanding he became. The Bible verse in Ephesians 5 about wives submitting to their husbands was enforced, but the husbands loving their wives as Christ loved the church was ignored. If I worked hard to get the laundry done, the kitchen cleaned, and the groceries bought, I was incompetent because I did not wash the floors. No matter how hard I worked to please him, things were never up to his standards. If I tried to confront him about his controlling and abusive behavior, he would quickly shut me up, insisting that I too was abusive, because I was defying him ... or that I only thought that because I was reading some f***** book that told me not to let a man tell me what to do. He made it quite clear that if I kept suggesting he was abusive, he would ignore me so much that I would become an insignificant part of his life. So much for a partnership in marriage.

If I were late for bed, I would get locked out of the bedroom. If I had a stain on my shirt and didn't notice, he would. Upon changing my shirt, he would ask why I wasn't wearing the other one. I was despised for not having an opinion, yet when I tried to have a voice, it would be stifled with profanity being hurled at me, or constant interruptions. Finally, I quit trying. His attacks were constant, no matter which way I turned. To say it became frustrating and debilitating is a gross understatement. Anxiety increased with each passing month. When I threatened to leave if things did not improve, we would have brighter patches. As he caught himself escalating, he'd backtrack, apologize, and we could discuss the situation somewhat rationally. Unfortunately, those happier days never lasted more than a few weeks. I began to feel like I lived my life at arm's length, disconnected from my heart, as daily life was far too painful.

I slid deeper into despair with the never ending battle on everything I did, thought, felt and said ... it's like slipping into oblivion ... after a while, I could no longer stand and fight. The worst form of control came near the end. On this particular night, we were fighting downstairs. Right at the point of his choice words of vulgarity, and his threat to "smash my head with a remote control" ... our son came down from his room. In a blaze of fury, Rob ran at the little guy, only four years old at the time, and chased him back to his room. An out-of-control spanking followed and I immediately stepped in to stop it. I was grabbed hard by my ribcage, dragged out of the room, and thrown into the wall. If I moved, I was told that I would get it worse. He went back into our son's room.

The ultimate power and control had been achieved. If I went in to rescue my child again, the kids could lose their mom; the one they needed to protect them. If I didn't, my little guy would take what was left of his wrath. It was a no-win situation. I thank God that his fury must have been abated, because nothing further happened. I finally realized, though, that his need for power and control was dangerously out of control. This scenario, and others like it, were part of the final escalation in the last year of our marriage. This type of control was intolerable, even for me, and it became one of the catalysts for me to finally break away.

Healing from this type of controlling behavior was difficult. I had trouble making even simple decisions. At first, I would always default to someone else's choice of restaurant or the destination for a walk. I had to seek a great deal of wise counsel for any major decisions. I felt a thick blackness over me that I believed even my prayers could not penetrate, so hearing from God was beyond me. I asked others to pray for me. They did, and soon I was able to start hearing direction from God on my own. Through this, He gave me a key to coming out from under the control of another person. This key is to surrender and submit my will, and everything else, to the Lord. It seems strange from a worldly standpoint; to heal from being controlled, instead of taking back our power and control, we give it away. It is the most profound and powerful way to live our lives. I felt the Lord telling me that He would take care of everything that I gave Him, so I eventually gave Him everything.

Learning to do this was a process. It did not happen all at once. God has shown me why we can't hang onto any pieces of the puzzle of our lives. You see, we don't see the big picture of the puzzle. The very pieces that we are hanging onto are the ones needed to be put in place in the way God sees it. Hanging onto any piece prevents them from being in their proper place, in the very place God designed them to be. Our holding onto things is leaving big gaps in the perfect plan, His perfect will for our life. He takes care of everything we give Him. So, we need to give Him everything; then He can and will take care of everything. As painful as this is at times, He knows so much better what to do with those pieces, the ones to which we so desperately try to hang onto. He knows how to take care of them. He sees the whole picture. He knows where those pieces need to go. How much better it is to hand over all the pieces of the puzzle of our lives to the One who sees the whole picture--backward, forwards, through time and space and all eternity! We don't need to understand, we only need to trust.

Piece by piece I handed it all over to Him and continue to do so today. With each new revelation, each new situation, each bump in the road, I came to understand how I was holding onto different pieces instead of giving them over to the control of the Father. Time, and time again, through prayer, I would hold another piece in my hands and offer it up to the Lord.

The biggest key was offering up my will to the Lord ... the things I wanted, the way I wanted things to go, the way I wanted my life to be ... my control over things. Then, as God revealed other areas, I surrendered them. From my kids, to my home, job, finances, burdens, heart, time, health, family, and this book ... I put them all in His hands and learned to trust. It is amazing how peaceful life can be, even in the midst of the storm, when the Lord is at the helm.

Through my journey in walking closely with Him and continual surrender, He has shown me that there are things He wants me to do-- my role, and things that He will do if I let Him--His role. He has spoken to my heart such things as these for me to do:

- *Trust Me.*
- *Walk with Me.*
- *Give me your time so I can give you My presence.*
- *Rest in Me. Rest in My embrace.*
- *Let go.*
- *Be Mine, fully Mine.*
- *Focus on Me.*
- *Stop striving.*
- *Depend on Me. Stay dependent.*
- *Rest in My peace. Rest in My presence. Be in My presence.*

- *Stop trying to figure it all out.*
- *Receive My grace.*
- *Speak life.*
- *Put your hope in Me.*
- *Put your faith in Me.*
- *Let Me reign in your heart.*
- *Fear no evil.*
- *See My ways.*
- *Hear My voice.*
- *Seek Me in all you do--in everything. See Me in all you do.*
- *Find Me in everything.*
- *Delight in Me.*
- *Keep surrendering.*
- *Share what you have learned; what I have shown you.*
- *Rejoice in all you do.*
- *Do not be anxious. Do not be afraid.*
- *Just worship. I will show you how to put on the war paint.*
- *Tell them about Me, about My love.*
- *Allow peace to flood your soul, your heart, your mind.*
- *Do not fight Me, rather walk along with Me in all things.*
- *Get out of the boat.*
- *Let Me be all things to you.*
- *Reach out and grasp My hand.*
- *Hang on to Me with both hands, let go of all that hinders you.*
- *Let go of all things hurting you.*

- *Revel in Me.*

- *Look into My eyes, see Me, know Me, find Me.*

- *The joy, love and peace you seek are yours as you seek Me.*

He has told me that He will do such things as these for me, or be such things as these for me as I surrender to Him:

- *I hold you in the palm of My hand.*

- *I will give you all you need.*

- *I will give you confident hope.*

- *I am restoring your hope.*

- *My grace is with you.*

- *My presence has all you need.*

- *I will guide you.*

- *My heart is for you.*

- *I will protect you.*

- *I will be on the path with you every step of the way.*

- *I will give you your dreams.*

- *I will put people in your path.*

- *I will change your circumstances.*

- *I will guide you in the path you should take.*

- *You will be blessed.*

- *You will be used of Me.*

- *Your heart will be taken care of.*

- *You will have My strength. I will strengthen you.*

- *I give you My peace.*
- *Chaos will come to order as you seek Me.*
- *You will know My presence is real, My intimacy is real.*
- *I will flood you with hope, with life, with love, with knowledge.*
- *I will help others through you.*
- *I will give you all the treasures you seek.*
- *All insecurities will fade away. You will step out confidently.*
- *I will give you the words as you seek Me.*
- *I am pouring out My life on you.*
- *I am pouring out My heart on you.*
- *I will pour out My spirit on you.*
- *I want you to live in full freedom.*
- *I will be your everything.*
- *I will be your husband.*
- *I will fill you with a love you could not have with another.*
- *You will experience richness from Me; seek nothing else.*
- *You will enter the glory realm.*
- *I will lead you step by step.*
- *I will make your life fun, joyous, full of freedom and peace.*
- *I am building trust.*
- *I am building hope.*
- *I am your song.*
- *I am there beside you, holding your hand.*
- *I am your provider, nurturer, lover, counselor, and giver of all joy, peace and life.*

- *I am all things to you.*
- *I am before you with My hand extended, reaching out in love.*
- *I am your stable foundation.*
- *I am the rock of your salvation.*
- *I will not fail.*
- *I will help you.*
- *My love never fails.*
- *My peace surrounds you like a shield.*
- *I will deliver you from all fear.*

Now, instead of living a life of following orders out of fear, my heart is at peace as I submit everything to Him, trust, and daily do all He asks of me. In this obedience and submission, He guides me and leads me to the paths I need to be on. I am willing and eager to follow the path He has set out for me, rather than choose my own. I have learned, from my experiences, that this is the better choice, both in the spiritual world and in the natural one.

In the natural world, I need constant direction ..., literally! I am admittedly directionally challenged. For the life of me, I cannot easily find my way around any place, no matter how big or small. From a shopping mall to a campground, parkade or on the highway, I retrace my steps many times over, make wrong turns, and end up heading in the opposite direction to what I need. The epitome of my directionless ways was when, arms loaded with shopping bags, and feet tired of treading, I asked my daughter to lead us back from the food court to our hotel that was attached to the mall. I knew she would take us in a straight path, and I physically and emotionally could not bear the meandering route I most assuredly would take. This would not be so remarkable ... but she was only six years old at the time, much to the amusement of the overhearing mall patrons! Even my GPS leaves me at dead ends, or frustrated and crying in a parking lot at an address that is supposed to exist yet seemingly does not!

I have learned that my life in the spirit is also like this. I often do not know the path to take, and am left floundering in the midst of it all. Thankfully, that is not what God has for me ... He is not directionally challenged! He knows our route, and He knows how to get us there, at the most opportune time. We just have to learn to listen. He says, "I will give you what you need just when you need it. That is why we walk together. I supply the needs as we come to circumstances and situations. I have the plan set. I know the way. I am your GPS!"

To come out from under the systematic control of someone, it is imperative that you break off all unhealthy soul-ties, to release you from that person in the spiritual realm. The soul refers to your mind, emotions, and will. A tie is anything that binds you, constricts you, or stops you from being who you are; it opens the door for the other person or thing to determine and dictate your actions, your thoughts, your feelings, your will and your choices. Let me stand beside you as you pray to break off these soul-ties that are negatively impacting your freedom, and your life.

Dear Heavenly Father,

I pray that You would show me where I have allowed myself to be bound and tied to a person, a thing, or an emotion that is unhealthy. Father, I ask that You would show me the people and the things from my past that I have given myself over to, and where I opened the door to control and abuse that has kept me bound. Lord, I now pray that You would cut off that spiritual tie that keeps me under its control, through which the unhealthiness flows. I pray that You allow only healthiness to flow in all my relationships--whether it be with a parent, child, spouse, close friend, or anyone or anything else, Lord, and that healing would come to both sides. Father, anything that I have allowed myself to be tied to that is not of You, Lord, I break it off in Jesus' name. I declare myself set free. I repent and renounce and break off all the behaviors that were brought on through that unhealthy soul tie, whether it was consciously, subconsciously, spiritually, known or unknown to me. Father, forgive me. I renounce the hardness of heart. I renounce all the fears. I renounce all addictions. I renounce anything that has kept me from Your joy, Your peace, and Your freedom. Now with the authority of the blood of Jesus and the finished work of the cross, and empowered by Holy Spirit, I break off all soul ties in Jesus' name.

Lord, in breaking these off, I pray for my soul; my mind, my will, and my emotions. I don't want to be bound to anything but you Lord. Father, Your Word is all about freedom. So I release any binding, and any unhealthiness from my life so that I can live in freedom.

I want, Father, to receive what You have for me, and Your Word says that I receive the mind of Christ. So, through Your Holy Spirit, please begin to renew my mind, my will, and my emotions, and bring healthiness to replace the lies and the unhealthiness. Thank You that You are healing, restoring and renewing my mind by the power of Holy Spirit. Lead me through Your Word, Lord. Guide me so that I may hear Your voice. By Your grace and empowerment, make Your Word alive to me. Make it that double-edged sword that would cut off anything on me that should not be there, all that is keeping me bound and under control.

I also break off, In Jesus' name, the spirit of mind control. I turn from and renounce any aspects of mind control that I have allowed into my life. I will no longer partner with it in any form. In its place, fill me with the mind of Christ, and the heart of the Father. I will no longer be controlled, but only be guided by Your voice, and Your wisdom, Lord, through the power of the Holy Spirt. I will walk freely in You, Lord. I pray all of this in Jesus' name.

Amen.

*T*hen Jesus said, "Come to me, all of you who are

weary and carry heavy burdens, and I will give you rest.

Matthew 11:28

*F*or I know the plans I have for you," says the Lord. "They are plans for good and not for disaster, to give you a future and a hope.

Jeremiah 29:11

*T*rust in the Lord with all your heart; do not depend on your own understanding. Seek his will in all you do, and he will show you which path to take.

Proverbs 3:5

*F*or, "Who can know the Lord's thoughts? Who knows enough to teach him?" but we understand these things, for we have the mind of Christ.

1 Corinthians 2:16

*F*or the word of God is alive and powerful. It is sharper than the sharpest two-edged sword, cutting between soul and spirit, between joint and marrow. It exposes our innermost thoughts and desires.

Hebrews 4:12

*H*e is so rich in kindness and grace that he purchased our freedom with the blood of his Son and forgave our sins.

Ephesians 1:7

Dear Child,

Let go of disappointment in all things. It is okay. You will have all you need. Let go of anger. You will have all you need. Let go of fear. You will have all you need. It comes down to TRUST. If you trust Me in everything, if you trust Me for everything, if you trust Me with everything … then you can let go of all those emotions that hinder you. You will find the peace among the chaos, among the storm. It all comes down to trusting Me. Waiting with false expectations creates tension. I do not want that for you. I want you to fall deeply into 'trust' with Me. The tension leads to not surrendering what I am asking you to surrender. It leads to heartache. It leads to false control, false hopes, false dreams. Fully let go and set your sights on what I have for you. Fully trust. Fully depend on, fully release. Then all will be truly well with your soul. You can rest. You can drink deeply, and this living water will go down into the depths of your soul, your heart, and give you the healing you long for, the grace you long for, the peace you long for. It will be from the depths of your heart then that true forgiveness, with the help of My Spirit, will flow. Peace will flow, love will flow, and you will love My people as I love you. Want this. Seek this. This is your journey. This is your calling. I want your heart. I want it full. I want it healed. I want it for My people, for My children. I want it all, and to do this, I need all of you.

♥ Jesus

The Hidden Places of my Heart

(So hidden, this chapter almost did not get written.)

I cannot blame God for my choice of husband, nor for all the traumatic repercussions that came with it. In my heart, I knew I was not to marry him ... I didn't even officially say, "Yes" to his proposal. I just didn't say, "No." My dad and my sister tried to warn me. I chose not to listen. Part of me thought that it would be okay. After all, I loved him and believed that if he ended up marrying me (I was not totally convinced he would show up for the wedding), that meant he was committed and really wanted to be with me. If he went through with it, then he must really love me ... so everything would eventually work out. Most other areas of my life turned out well so why wouldn't this?

"Besides," I thought, "we had broken up several times during the relationship, once even quite close to the wedding date-- invitations had already been sent! If I was not to marry him, wouldn't I feel a tremendous amount of relief at our breakup, rather than this "on the floor kind of pain?" I know now that the unbearable pain was from unbroken soul ties. Once you become intimate with someone your souls are connected (Genesis 2:24). When the united souls are separated, there is a ripping apart of those souls, causing great anguish. These soul ties must be broken (See Under Control) before you can move forward.

The other part of me that allowed this walk in disobedience to continue was the part that was angry at God. I was frustrated that at 28 years old, He had not yet sent me the strong Christian husband that I had believed I would have had by now ... after all, I had been serving the Lord somewhat faithfully for more than ten years now, and I was ready, I thought. I was getting older and older, and my single friends were getting younger and younger, and now even they were getting married. I had been distancing myself from my church family for some time as I started to feel more, and more betrayed by God for not giving me what I wanted. I began to be jealous of all those young people around me who were starting their families, so in love and happy ... and here I was, still alone, walking into each church function by myself. I began to see myself as unwanted ... the unchosen one. I disconnected even more and drifted farther and farther from God. I soon began to date a close friend that I had known for years from university. Eventually, as much as he loved me, he broke it off. Ironically, it was because I was a Christian and he was not. I believe he knew God had so much more for me and he knew he couldn't be it. He was so much stronger than I. To this day I have a tremendous amount of respect for him.

Turning away from God instead of towards Him in this confusion, anger, and rebellion, I opened the door that allowed me to make unwise decisions and unholy choices that would eventually lead me down a path of my own destruction. That was when I met Rob. I fell quickly to the charms of a narcissist as he spun his web around me. Very shortly into the relationship, after saving myself for my husband all these years, I fell. At that point, I bought into the lie that

"I had made my bed, and now I had to lie in it." Shame, guilt, and condemnation flooded me, and I allowed them to steal my life. In attempts to rationalize and justify my sin and guilt, I made myself believe that at least if I married him I would have still saved myself for my husband. Technically, he still would be the only one with whom I had been with in biblical terms.

More shame and guilt crept in throughout the marriage as I realized how desperate my situation was becoming. I felt, for the first time in my life, utterly powerless to stop it. My shame and guilt continually whispered to me that because I had been disobedient to God I could not go to Him to help me get out of it. These lies kept me bound in a relationship that almost destroyed me. It would take me over twenty years to climb out of the black pit of hell it put me in. Now it has led me to dedicate my life to try and help release anyone else who is suffering, suffocating, and drowning in an abusive relationship. So now, dear Reader, I am going to tell you what your mom, your dad, your sister, your friend ... whoever ... is trying to tell you, but you are not listening because you believe that they just don't understand ... that they just don't get it. Well, I know. I understand. Too well. I lived it. I was there. I walked through it. I barely survived to tell about it. It almost killed me. Thankfully I did survive, and God is now asking me to tell you about it. He wants you to hear this and listen with your whole heart.

Think of a small child, running, their arms up, a giggle of excitement spilling out of them, trust in their eyes, fully expecting to be picked up and swung around in delight! Instead, a hand comes down and slaps them. Harsh words slam into their bodies. They are pushed down again, and again. Maybe they are even savagely beaten or raped. Perhaps they are brutally murdered. This is what your mom sees. This is what your dad, your sister, your friend ... all those ones who care about you and love you, see. This is what God the Father sees. This is the reality, or will be the reality. It always gets worse. You may not see it, or believe it. Nevertheless, it is the truth. Do not let the deception of the enemy, the deception of shame, guilt and condemnation trap you into living a life that is not meant for you. God has so much more for you than this. Do not let it keep you in a relationship that will kill some part of you, one way or another. See the reality of what you are in, or were in. Understand what it is doing to you. Stop believing the lies that it will be all right, or that it will justify any choices you have made or anything you have done. Maybe you are believing the lie that, "I made my bed, now I have to lie in it," that you had brought this type of life on yourself, that you somehow deserved it, and now had to live with it. Yes, maybe you have made mistakes but living in abuse does not make anything right. God is a God of many chances. God's kindness leads to repentance. Repentance and surrender allow us to change the direction of our lives. We do not have to continue down a path of destruction.

No, God does not want this for you. He wants to bathe you, wash away the blood and put healing ointment on you. He wants to clothe you in fine linen, cover you with costly garments, and adorn you with jewelry. He wants to help you rise to be the queen He created you to be (Ezekiel 16:9-14). He crowns you with glory and honor (Psalm 8:5). This is the picture of life God wants to give you; one of royalty, beauty, and brilliance--where you are the precious child of the King. The Lord is calling out to you and saying: "Hold on to Me with both hands. When you have both hands on Me, you cannot hold on to anything else. Surrender to Me, My darling. Look at Me. Look at My eyes. See My love for you. See My hope for you. See My dream for you. Do not let go. I am holding onto You with both hands and holding you close. Have no fear. I will not let you fall. I am holding you tight, comforting you, drawing you near. I catch your tears as they fall. I have always done so. Release this deep sadness to Me. I am washing you clean, cleansing your heart, purifying you. You are My bride.

This is the life the Father wants to give you. Sadly, the enemy uses shame, guilt and condemnation to try to steal your identity. He is trying to steal your future like he tried to steal mine. As long as the shame stays hidden in those secret places of our hearts, it has power over us. As long as we believe that we cannot--will not--think about it, let alone speak about it, that we must keep it in the dark because it is too bad, too ugly, nobody will understand or love us if they know about it; it will continue to have a death grip on our lives. But once we bring the shame out of the dark and expose it, it loses all power. It is the secrecy that allows it to stay, and as long as it is allowed to stay, it is doing its hidden damage. Though even the thought of facing and voicing our shame may hurt incredibly, like a seemingly insignificant sliver hiding in our hand, it will only get worse if we leave it in and cover it up. Infection and poison eventually set in and soon it is affecting our entire bodies and wrecking our entire lives.

Instead, we need to trust our shame, no matter how painful, to the Father. Confess it to Him. Begin speaking out all those secret things that we do not want anyone to know. He is faithful and just, and He alone can remove it. He will remove it gently and in love. Whether the shame, guilt, and condemnation entered through a mistake in our lives, whether we contributed to it in some way, knowingly or unknowingly, willingly or unwillingly, or whether it was in total innocence, we still need to offer it up to the Lord. He wants us to bring it to Him for our benefit, not to bring more shame, nor judge, criticize or belittle us. Then we need to trust that the temporary pain that comes in rooting out the shame will lead to our ultimate healing. That is when we can be set free and begin to heal those secret, painful places of our hearts. That is when we can start to be the person God created us to be--free to sing, dance, laugh, and love.

Please give me the honor of praying with you as you ask God to cleanse you from any shame, guilt, and condemnation that are rooted deep in the hidden places of your heart.

Dear Heavenly Father,

I come before You on my knees, with my head lowered, unable to even look up to You. I know I can no longer live like this; it hurts too much. I need You to come and expose those secret places of my heart, those deep places of pain that I have kept hidden--the ones that I don't want to admit even to myself. Help me to be willing to release all of it to You, that which I know, and that which You reveal. Help me to trust You with those dark secrets, and know that You will be gentle in the healing of my vulnerable heart. Holy Spirit, help my spirit rise up and ward off any lies coming at me, screaming that it must stay hidden. Shame keeps things in the dark. Shame doesn't go to the Father.

Shame doesn't confess. Shame wraps, conceals, and numbs the heart, keeping it in its pain. **But I say, "NO!" It must be revealed.** *All* of my heart must be revealed for *all* of my heart to be healed. I know, Father, this is the only way I can truly be free and walk tall, with my head held high.

So I ask Holy Spirit to reveal all the roots of shame, guilt and condemnation so that I may offer them all up to You to be healed--body, soul, and spirit. Please give me the courage I need to do this... You know all of them anyway for nothing in all creation is hidden from You ... yet You still love me. (Continue to wait as Holy Spirit reveals any roots of shame, guilt and condemnation.)

Lord, I give you _____ (speak out all that is on your heart and anything the Lord has revealed to you.) Please take these from me and release me from all the shame, guilt and condemnation associated with them, and any effects and results they have had on me in any capacity, known or unknown, now or in the past. Lord, if I have believed any lies that "I have made my bed, and now I have to lie in it," "It was my mistake, so I have to live with it," "I was disobedient, so God won't help me," or "_____" (name any other lie), I pray that You break it off of me right now and fill my heart with Your truth. Please forgive me for partnering with that lie in any way. Thank you, Lord, for removing all my guilt and shame, healing all those deep places of my heart, and filling them with Your oil of joy, peace, freedom, and the righteousness of Christ.

Thank You, Lord, that it is never too late to turn around and change paths, even if I have chosen the path. Like the prodigal son, You will welcome me back with open arms. With Your mercy and grace, lead me to repent in any other areas that I need to do so. Thank You that through repentance, I receive forgiveness and freedom from shame.

Thank You that You do not hold any of my decisions against me, but redeem them, giving me beauty for ashes.

Please, Lord, help me to forgive myself. I come against any shame, guilt, condemnation or judgments that I have put on myself, or that were put on me by the enemy, or by anyone else in my life because of my past. I break off the fear, the humiliation, the criticism, the disgust, and the contempt that was attached to every shameful word spoken over me. I command those things to be loosed off of me so that they would not have the power to form my identity. I pray that my identity would instead be found in You, as the child of the Most High God, one who is redeemed into a royal family, with all the inheritance and all the attributes of a royal family. God, I pray that You would set Your crown on my head today, and that every feeling of shame, disgust, and humiliation would go, and that I would walk in the robes of righteousness and under the crown that You have placed on my head, with my head held high, knowing who I am. I take authority over the spirit of shame, and in the name of Jesus, I command you, and every word that you have spoken against me, to go, and that and every part of me that has been bound in shame be set free. I pray that my mind, my emotions, and my body be healed and set completely free by the Prince of Peace.

Lord, I thank You that during Your time on earth, You honored the women who others accused and condemned. You released them from their bondage and shame, like the woman who was caught in adultery and brought before you to be stoned. You sent her accusers away with the words, "... let the one who has never sinned throw the first stone!" There was not one person left standing there that could judge or condemn her. Jesus, You released her, and took away her shame, giving her a simple command, "Go and sin no more."

Thank You, Lord, that You do not accuse me nor condemn me. You do not want me to continue to live in any shame, but have draped me in a robe of righteousness. You have removed my sins as far from me as the East is from the West, and I have become righteous through faith in Christ. I ask You, Lord, that You turn around what the enemy has meant for evil, and use it for Your good. Thank You for the water of Your spirit that washes over me, and Your Word, that cleanses my soul. I pray this all in Jesus' mighty name. I can now, truly, walk tall, with my head held high.

Amen

He has removed our sins as far from us as the East is from the West.

Psalm 103:12

...*What* are mere mortals that you should think about them, human beings that you should care for them? Yet you made them only a little lower than God and crowned them with glory and honor.

Psalm 8:4-5

*I*nstead of shame and dishonor, you will enjoy a double share of honor. You will possess a double portion of prosperity in your land, and everlasting joy will be yours.

Isaiah 61:7

I am overwhelmed with joy in the Lord my God! For he has dressed me with the clothing of salvation and draped me in a robe of righteousness. I am like a bridegroom dressed for his wedding or a bride with her jewels.

Isaiah 61:10

I no longer count on my own righteousness through obeying the law; rather, I become righteous through faith in Christ. For God's way of making us right with himself depends on faith.

Philippians 3:9

"When he finally came to his senses, he said to himself, 'At home even the hired servants have food enough to spare, and here I am dying of hunger! I will go home to my father and say, "Father, I have sinned against both heaven and you, and I am no longer worthy of being called your son. Please take me on as a hired servant." So he returned home to his father. And while he was still a long way off, his father saw him coming. Filled with love and compassion, he ran to his son, embraced him, and kissed him. His son said to him, 'Father, I have sinned against both heaven and you, and I am no longer worthy of being called your son. "But his father said to the servants, 'Quick! Bring the finest robe in the house and put it on him. Get a ring for his finger and sandals for his feet. And kill the calf we have been fattening. We must celebrate with a feast, for this son of mine was dead and has now returned to life. He was lost, but now he is found.' So the party began.

Luke 15:17-24

Dear Child,

I will shine on you as you seek My face. My eyes gaze on you in love. Don't pay mind to what others say about you. Though your enemies persecute you, I am strong in you. We walk together. I will not leave you. My love reigns in your heart. I love gazing upon you. You are a precious treasure in My sight. You are not valueless. You are precious. Stay close to Me. I will fill you. I will fill your heart. I will love you always. Do not let go of My hand. Trust My Word. Trust the voice of My spirit. I will lead and guide you.

♥ Jesus

Part 3

Now What?

Moving Forward

The Call to Warrior

I had two interventions while living in the cycle of abuse. The first was not too long into the marriage. I had run into some people I knew in my "previous life" from where I used to live. From that chance meeting, word got back to my friends, the question being "What's up with Calli? She looks like hell." They drove up and took me out for supper. I did disclose some things, but I was not yet ready to make any changes.

The second intervention was with a group of women from my church, many years later though I don't remember the actual timeline. I talked a little, but mostly they prayed for me. In the end, I was praying with just my closest friend and I heard a voice, not quite audible, but so strong in my spirit and so out of nowhere that I looked around for who could have voiced it. It said: "You are not a mouse in this. Stand up and be a WARRIOR!" God had called me out and given me a command. I was to be a warrior. I was to fight … only I didn't know how.

But that is the amazing thing about God … I did not have to figure it all out then, and I do not have to figure it all out now. I didn't have to strive or even understand what it would take to stop being the cowering woman I had become and start being one of the someones who could help lead the charge, shoulder to shoulder with the Lord Jesus. No, I did not have to know it all; my role was to seek Him with trust and obedience, and to find out who He was for me in the middle of my mess.

My biggest need in the beginning stages of my healing journey was for peace within the chaos that went on in my life, even after I had left … not just learning to dance in the rain, but to dance, thrive and rejoice amidst the storms still raging. And slowly, I did. Recently, my sister gave me a plaque that celebrated my ability to dance in the rain … she knew I had earned that badge! I cannot even describe how I finally received peace … just that slowly, as God healed me, transformed my heart, renewed my mind and flipped my perspective of everything on its head, He also taught me to use my faith in Him as a shield to protect me from the attacks that were still launched at me. I no longer had to defend myself. God did it for me. The words Rob still throws at me continue to sting, but the impact of them is no longer causing deep wounds. I will have no more scars from them.

At one time, I had thought that I would know I was healed when his words no longer hurt. That is not so. That would only happen if I were so closed off emotionally that I no longer felt anything; pain or joy. I do not want that. Now I know that I am healed not because I no longer get hurt, but because while I feel the pain I let it go quickly before it cuts deep into my heart. The words no longer haunt me. The pain used to last for months, even years; now it is only a flicker … that is all part of learning to dance in the storm and maintain peace of mind and heart.

My other biggest need at the time was the fight against the loneliness that constantly crept in. However, soon God brought me a friend that would change that part of my journey. She brought so much more to my life than just company. We spent a great amount of time together and she poured many powerful prayers into my life. She would be the one to see God making something beautiful out of the emotional scars I carried across my chest. When I first told her of my situation, her words were something like "I don't know what to do about that ... but we can pray." And pray we did. It became the cornerstone of our friendship. She taught me to go to the Lord in prayer for everything ... prayer changes things. She was the type of friend that would carry me when I went into my shocked numb state after yet another attack from Rob (before I had learned how critical it was not to engage in, respond to, or defend myself in the attack). God used her to open up other doors in my life as well. She encouraged me to submit my resumé for my current job. This became a huge support in my healing process. She also introduced me to my house church and two more mentors whom I soon would learn to trust and grow to love. They would, in turn, cover me in prayer, teach me about the love of Jesus, and constantly encourage me as I struggled to rebuild my life.

Their house church would meet to worship with instruments and voices each week. Every week as they worshiped, I would sit curled up under a counter, back to the wall, in a position of safety and security ... so broken ... and weep. Some of the people wondered what was wrong with me, but they gave me the space that I needed to allow God to heal me as I let their worship flood over me for the next year, maybe two. I was able to participate and worship more, and more, and soon the tears of trauma stopped altogether. For a while, I was just able to worship, finding true joy. Then the tears started again, stronger than ever before ... but only when the worship reflected a battle cry ... the Lord calling up His warriors ... and I was reminded of that call of the Lord, from years before. Now my tears were calling me to rise, to fight for my kids, to fight the battle for others coming through what I was being given victory over … to be the warrior God was commanding me to be.

By this time I had already taken a course (twice) at Family Services on domestic violence, also the Divorce Care course at my church, and had completed the first level of The Genesis Process, a course designed to facilitate healing of inner wounds. I felt like I was finally able to get out of the "hospital bed," but was facing the "now what?" I had finally healed enough to feel like I could start moving forward again, but was struggling with knowing where to go and what to do. I still thought that I had to figure it all out; that I still had to make the entire plan that would map out my future … the one I finally believed I had.

Soon, the opportunity came to go to family camp with my church organization. One of the speakers was a lady who pastored a church in Calgary with her husband. She was a strong believer in the sanctity of the family. Heartbroken and feeling the guilt of being part of a broken family, I went to her for prayer. Thinking I was going to be condemned and encouraged to "try again," she surprised me. She acknowledged that I was being hurt over, and over again. My relationship was in no way safe, mentally or physically, so it was without question that God would not want me in a relationship where I was not safe in my own home. I had previously heard from my pastor that my vows … to love, honor, and cherish … had already been broken. I was not breaking my vows by leaving. They were already broken. You cannot break something that's already broken. Her confirmation of that, and her prayers for me, gave me the release I needed to finally let go of the false guilt and condemnation I was still feeling. It gave me the release I needed to continue to move forward, instead of always looking back in guilt and doubt. I still fall back on this old guilt, briefly, when my children are showing their pain. But I know I did what I had to do, and am still doing what I have to do … I cannot even imagine how damaged I would be today if I had not … my healing journey, my call to a warrior, and this book would not even exist. I am not sure I would even exist. But they do, and so do I, and I was finally ready to start moving forward.

While I was struggling with the "Now What," God led me to a weekend retreat put on by my church. I was not planning to go, as none of "my people" were going. Fortunately, a girl I didn't know too well at the time said, "I've got your back," and that she'd go with me. There, God spoke to me, and spoke to me, and spoke to me, through different people, scriptures, prophetic words, and song. It amazed me how clearly the Lord gave me His message. I could not possibly have missed it! One friend even jokingly commented: "This is all for you! The rest of us may as well go home!"

A prophetic word was given by a participant that set the tone for the retreat. She said she felt like some of us were still huddled under our umbrellas, even though the storm had passed … "Your spring is here," she encouraged us, "step out and embrace it." That word resonated deeply in my spirit. I felt like that was exactly where I was at. Next came a prophetic song from my new friend that touched my heart. She confirmed it by later telling me that she was thinking of me when she sang it … others too, but it was definitely for me. The speaker then gave her message. Part of it was based on Song of Songs 2:11-12: Look, the winter is passed, and the rains are over and gone. The flowers are springing up; the seasons of singing birds has come…" This verse had been given to me by my friend several months previous, and it was in my birthday card from my daughter. It was, therefore, the verse I had chosen for that year, helping me to believe God's promise to me that my long, long, season of difficulty was indeed, coming to an end; there would be new life and brightness coming into my journey in the days ahead. The storms and tumultuous days were finally over for me ... I could indeed move on. As the speaker finished her message, she had the worship leader begin to play the song "Come to Me," by Bethel ... the same song that a friend suggested I listen to ... and listen to it I did ... over, and over again as I sat by the water fountain in my garden and cried. It was a very healing song for me.

After listening to it in amazement for a bit, I knew beyond all doubt that I needed to respond to the altar call. I went forward for prayer. Immediately, the wife of our lead pastor came and wanted to pray with me. She said she knew she would be praying for me, so she wanted to get the notes she had written! Since I hadn't come up for prayer right away, she had left them at her table, but my response, though belated, was confirmation that what she had written was indeed for me. At this point, I had never spoken to her about my struggle with the "what now" and the trying to figure out God's plan for my life. Even so, her notes said:

My hands are in front of me

facing upwards to your throne

open and vulnerable

with nothing left to hide.

God, what is your plan for me now?

Your plan is to heal,

Your plan is to ...

From there she went on to say that God will put steps in front of me, and I would just have to obedient and do the little things that He asked me to do. That was all I had to do ... I didn't have to see anything beyond that. She was crying as she spoke to me (and it is well known that she rarely cries), and so was I ... I knew this was from the Lord in answer to my burning question--to guide me and show me the plan--reassuring me that I did not have to figure it all out right then. I still don't have to figure it all out. I just have to take that one small step of faith and do the very next thing that He asks me to do. That is all; no more, no less. It brought to mind a drawing my sister had done for me years previous--a little girl holding a lantern. The light shone only far enough ahead to light the way for one step ...

As I sat back down, my new friend gave me the prophetic words she was given for me as she saw me at the altar:

> Calli, you have something to offer because I'm in you.
>
> I see your hurt and your pain, but My blood covers all and makes you whole.
>
> In everything, choose to pursue Me.
>
> I have not called you to fix everything, but to put your trust in Me.

... and that was enough to put my heart at rest. My path was set before me. It was not as complicated as I tried to make it. I just had to worship the Lord and set my heart on pursuing Him. I had to trust Him and be obedient in all He put before me no matter how big or small. At first I was not sure I would recognize the steps He wanted me to take, but I soon came to understand how it worked. Very soon after the retreat I heard the announcement for the start of the new

Cleansing Stream Class. I had always thought that I should take the class … but this time there was no thought … I just knew, without question, that I was to be in that class. It was the next step the Lord wanted me to take. With it, came much healing--such a deep level of healing in areas that I did not even know I was still so wounded. It was the healing that I needed to take me from being a soldier for the Lord, to being a warrior for Him.

In this class, I met the most amazing prayer warriors and anointers--people who loved God, and who knew how to fight with Him in battle and bring healing and freedom to people's lives. They have become my closest friends and prayer partners. I do not know what I would do without them. I enrolled in the class--twice--and I couldn't leave. God led me to be on the ministry team and help others now heal their wounds.

From there, God continued to put steps in front of me … and I had to take each one faithfully. Slowly, I kept changing and continued to heal and gain more, and more freedom. Gone were the "cliffs and storms" and the "weeping, broken woman" from the past prophetic words that had been spoken over me. The new words were that I would become "God's firm, straight arrow that would hit the mark even when things were coming against it," "a deliverer of hope," and " a person of freedom; a person that brings freedom to other people's lives."

I am still learning to walk out the destiny in which the Lord has called me. I do not know where I'll be going, or exactly what I'll be doing in my future. That no longer matters. He constantly showers His love and blessings on me, teaches me, and guides me. I still only see far enough ahead to just take the next step or maybe two. But the

Lord has shown me that there is a reason it's called walking out your destiny. The natural tendency for some of us is to want to arrive "Now!"... or at least know in advance what our destiny holds. God the Father knows better. He leads and guides us step by step, one thing at a time, one truth at a time, one revelation at a time. Too fast and we would not grow and learn the things that are essential to our development, thus thwarting our ability to perform in all the ways that our destiny requires. Things must build slowly, on a firm foundation. New truths, skills, abilities, wisdom, knowledge, insights, relationships, depth of character, spiritual revelations, and circumstances are formed with each footstep. Sometimes we backtrack and wander in circles to practice those new skills or ensure the new truths are deeply embedded. Each new challenge God puts in our path causes us to develop and change, making us that much stronger for the next obstacle; pulling us up to a higher spiritual dimension.

Sometimes, even knowing too much about our destiny too far ahead of time can be detrimental as we may become scared or overwhelmed, thinking, "How am I going to be able to do that?" It would be like thinking we had to jump over the mountain in one giant leap, not seeing that God has already prepared each step for the journey to be taken one at a time--no tremendous leaping required!

Or, we may be so excited that we run ahead of God, trying to do it our way, possibly taking shortcuts, and missing many of the necessary twists and turns that are needed to accomplish God's ultimate purposes. If we follow the trail God gives us, by the time we begin walking in our destiny we are no longer the same person we were as we started out at the long, seemingly impossible road ahead. What would not have been even possible for us all that time ago, is now just another regular routine step with God that no longer seems unfathomable. We step into it naturally, totally undaunted, knowing we are perfectly capable of taking that one step ...

So when we get anxious and restless to know all that lies ahead, or fear we will not be able to walk fully out what we have been called into, remember that in our trust and obedience, God will take us exactly where we need to go--whether we know it or not. Though we are not able to scale that mountain in one giant leap, we can take one "God-directed" step. That is all that is required ... one small step in trust and obedience, and He will do the rest.

*N*ow our knowledge is partial and incomplete, and even the gift of prophecy reveals only part of the whole picture! Now we see things imperfectly, like puzzling reflections in a mirror, but then we will see everything with perfect clarity. All that I know now is partial and incomplete, but then I will know everything completely, just as God now knows me completely.

1 Corinthians 13:9, 12

Dear Child,

Are you ready for more? That will come as you spend more, and more time seeking Me, in My presence, learning about Me, chasing My heart. Our hearts will become more, and more connected. You will have more, and more peace and wisdom as you spend more, and more time with Me. I cannot pour My heart into yours unless it is wholly available. Lift up My name in all you do. Do not be ashamed. Proclaim what I have done for you. That is what it is about--My love for My people and My healing grace. That is what people need, what they seek, what they want. Plug into Me, be energized through time with Me. It is better than any other source of power. I am your way, your truth, your life. I am the life all are seeking. I am all you need. I am all you want. Every need is met through Me. Eternal life is yours. I hold out My hand and offer it to you as you seek Me, as you trust Me, as you earnestly pursue Me with all you have … your time, resources, money, life … I am all you need. Trust. Relax. Have fun. It will be okay. You will shine and be shiny once again. You will see!

♥Jesus

The Pen – Released to Write

Another step of my healing journey led me to take an Elijah House course for healing trauma. During prayer ministry after one session, God brought to remembrance one particular assault that seemed key in my healing. Though it was not one that left me with any physical scars or even bruises, it was one that left its mark of terror entrenched deep in my heart. I can't even remember the circumstances of the incident, but it resulted in me being up against the kitchen counter, leaning over backward as far as I could go, frozen in absolute terror. Rob was holding a pen an inch from my eye while he was in an extreme rage. I can't remember if he was yelling harsh words, threatening me, or just letting the physical act itself yell loudly into my soul. What I do remember is being too scared to move, to say anything, or to even breathe, fully realizing that in the next few moments I could be blinded or have that pen shoved right through my eye into my brain.

At that point, the woman praying with me stopped and asked "Why the pen? Why the pen?"

I snapped back, "Because he wanted to terrify me, and the pen happened to be there!" (His weapons of choice always seemed to be whatever was handy--a golf club, a remote control, a water glass …)

"No, no," she said, "why the pen?" God later showed me in my spirit, exactly "why the pen."

Jesus took that pen out of his hand, put it in my hand, and said, "Now write!"

During that course, my friends were praying for me and in the spirit, one of them saw a wall surrounding me, with the word silence on it. I was coming to realize that many defenses had been placed around me to keep me shut up; to keep me from having a voice about all I had learned through my many years of trials. They prayed to release me from the wall of silence that was blocking me from speaking out and from writing the things that God wanted me to write.

I would find out six months later, that one friend went home that night and immediately was sick. God asked her if she was willing to be sick for Calli. She said, "Yes," and did not take any medication. She threw up every half hour, all night long. I do not know what happened in the spiritual realm that night, but something was broken; something was released by her obedience and her willingness to stand with me.

On January 31, 2015, after more prayers with a warrior friend, I had a breakthrough. I was given complete freedom and release to speak out and write about everything God had taught me. God then commissioned me to write prophetically, sharing His heart for His people, and to share my story. I was a captive, set free by His love and grace, and now He wanted me to share my story with others.

My Commission – January 31, 2015

I will give you the words, just write. I made you a writer to write My heart. Trust and you will see. Take that one step of faith; from that mustard seed of faith the words will flow, and I will paint pictures in people's hearts through words that are Mine, not your own, but you will be My hand, My heart, My love to My people. Trust and you will see. Only trust. I care about My people, and I need them to see that. You are an extension of My hand, My heart to My people. Your words will touch their hearts, their minds, their lives, their very souls. They will cry out to Me and I will show them My love. I will shower them with blessings. I will shine forth in their lives like never before.

Conclusion

What the f*** did you do now? (love). It's such a waste of time being married to an educated woman! (respect). You need to be humiliated! (joy). Treating you like this is a conscious decision. I will keep treating you like this until you get the message (honor). I only don't beat you because I don't want to (loyalty). I'll throw you off the balcony (Until death do us part). Maybe death will not be that far off.

I believed that at one point in my life. However, it does not have to come to that. You do have a choice. Violence--so far away from what I had experienced growing up. Abuse--so far from what I expected would be the focus of my life for so many years. It became the life I had been living and it had been all consuming, trying to suck every bit of energy and vitality from my being. At one time I had thought, "Maybe I'm blowing this all out of proportion. Maybe it's not as bad as I think it is. Maybe I'm making a big deal out of nothing." Now I know these are his words, not mine. Maybe I could have survived. Maybe life should be about more than survival. What happened to love and loyalty, joy and peace, trust and respect? Living in it, my perspective of relationships became warped. I was excited when he was kind to me, but my friends would say, "What is the big deal, Calli, that is normal!" That was my reality check.

I had to find out what a normal life was like again. I realized that violence and abuse do not have to be my normal any longer; it did not have to be my life. I stopped being the victim and started being the survivor. And now, God has called me to move past even that and be the warrior to fight for and with those still in the battle, to share what I've learned, and to make their walk, I pray, a little bit easier.

Over the years, I have learned to be aware of many of the common characteristics in the profile of the batterer. I had noticed the behavior and coined the phrase "Dr. Jekyll and Mr. Hyde" personality long before I started reading it in the literature. I was also keenly aware of the strong need for the abuser to control his wife in a way that he would control his possessions. I knew well his contradicting characteristics of being suspicious, moody, tense, and terrifying, yet insecure, needy, and fearful of inadequacy. However, when I read further into this area, I discovered his behavior is not beyond his control. I used to rationalize his behavior, thinking and believing that he could not control himself. I began to realize his behavior was not only very controlled but also very calculated. He had his reasons and would delude not only me, but himself into believing his actions and behaviors were rational.

I also had thought it was unique that my abuser believed he knew my motivations (or ulterior motives) behind my every action, and my feelings in every situation. This too, is typical. This allows him to have that inner conversation, started with an innocent comment, and escalating within his head until the situation triggers a hostile reaction. At first I could never understand how a simple comment or action could become the basis for such a violent argument, or cause such a misunderstanding. I understand it now. It was not necessarily what I had said, or even how I said it, but what he perceived as my "underhanded motivation" behind it. Then, the resulting argument he had not with me, but with himself, escalated it to the point of insanity. I now realize that it is not anything I had done, or what I had said, or even how I said it that has caused the situation. I had no control over his reactions or decisions, and no matter how I changed the dance (a phrase used by one of my counselors), the situation would never become rational.

No matter how obviously logical I thought things were, I could not make him see or understand the logic in it by what I said. This is a hard thing to overcome. Since the world of an abusive relationship defies logic and rational thinking, dealing with it in what seems a rational or obvious way does not work, will not work, cannot work, as there are no logical cause and effect relationships in the entire situation. In other words, you cannot use logic or reason to make the abuser stop, because nothing about the entire situation is logical or reasonable. The victim never made the abuser start, so she cannot make him stop.

Coming to this realization was a monumental enlightenment for me. It took away that intense feeling of "if only I can talk to him and make him see, make him understand ... it's not what he thinks ... I never meant it like that ... why can't he see I was only trying to ... that was not why I ... I wasn't thinking that ..." They do not believe you know how you were feeling or what you were thinking. They believe only they know what you were feeling and thinking, and why you did what you did. When the information they believe is inaccurate (which is probably always the case), it is incredibly frustrating and leaves you questioning yourself about how you can be so inadequate that you cannot make him understand. You have to realize that changing the dance--changing what you are doing or not doing, or how you react or do not react--will not matter. It will not change anything. It will never change anything. You do not have to change anything. You cannot make him change. You cannot make him see, or make him understand. You are not the one with the problem. He is.

However, another seemingly contradictory realization I came to was that the batterer is not, in fact, the one with the problem! You are! What he seeks are power and control. What he gets are power and control. He does not have a problem. He gets what he is after. Why would he want to change? In reality, it is the person being dominated, the person being hurt and stepped on time, and time again, that has the problem. She is the one who needs to take drastic action to change the situation, remembering that while she can change the *situation*, (GET OUT!) she cannot change *him*.

During my university counseling class many years ago, I searched the resource material for common denominators in victimization. I noticed the literature was careful to avoid giving a profile for fear of perpetuating the "blame the victim" scenario. One resource did specify that there may be issues of low self-esteem to begin with, or one that has been damaged temporarily by specific events, leaving them vulnerable at certain times of their lives. As well, it was explained to me that there may be different esteems for different areas of your life, making you confident is some areas, and vulnerable in others. These new ideas helped me to reconcile a dilemma within me about my situation, for I could not understand how I could be a "typical abuse victim," when in my professional life and other areas of my personal life, I was viewed as a strong, confident, independent woman.

I have known for a while how traumatizing it is for children to be abused, as I have lived with the result for several years, but I had not realized it is just as devastating for children who witness abuse. It is a myth that it is better for the children if the mother keeps the family together at all costs, especially if she believes they are not being affected, since they are not the ones being abused. By not breaking the cycle, the behavior will be deemed acceptable, and this will become the model of relationships for the children. Consequently, the abuse will be continued by the next generation.

I was very thankful that I had kept a journal through my ordeal, even though it was sporadic. It helped me keep my sanity when he started the crazy-making abuse of "pulling stunts" and then denying them, suggesting I was the crazy one, or the one who needed professional help. It helped me share my ordeal with others and validated my experiences. It made my situation more real and helped me to acknowledge the truth and the reality of my turbulent life. As I sat alone, deciding whether to stay or not, and reread my journals, though it was hard to read, even for me, it helped me not forget what I had been through, and how severe it was. Most of the events are burned into my brain, but seeing it in black and white makes it more real. I had to admit how bad it was. It helped me face reality and made me more secure in my decisions. As I faced the loneliness after I left, it reminded me of why I left. It reminded me that yes, it really was that bad. I am still discovering the long lasting effects it had on who I was as a person, who I had become, and who I am now.

The effects of abuse on the survivor are severe. I am only too painfully aware of what those effects are. The minimization of events, the high tolerance for danger and degradation, the shame, the shell shock, the hyper-vigilance to avoid displeasing the abuser, the normalization of horrific situations, and use of destructive coping strategies are only a small part of what I had to understand. I had heard far too often how I was being fractured as a person and that I would lose all of my identity if I did not get out soon, and the longer I stayed in it, the more of me I would lose. But it has only been recently that I have come to understand how close I was to death emotionally, mentally and physically. Head knowledge and heart knowledge are so far apart. You can list the effects by heart, or tell them to others in a bad situation, but when it is you, it is totally different. Everything can be justified and rationalized, right into the grave. The longer you are in it, the more skewed your perspective, or sense of the norm, gets. The more hurt you become, the more you try to defend, the more you try to hide, the more you try to protect those around you by lying and saying everything is okay. You do not want people to see your pain for fear they will either be judgmental of you or that they will hurt too, by witnessing what you are going through. You do not wish to cause any more pain than the pain you are already causing by continually failing to meet the needs of someone you love. (Only after do you realize that you cannot meet his needs, for if he needed the light on, and you turned it on, then he would have needed the light off.) What more can be said? You live in survival mode. That is not life. Only you do not know that it is not life. For it is your life. It is what you know.

But you can change it for you and your children. You must change it in order to survive while you are still somewhat you. Leaving is a process and it may take more than one time to make it out successfully. I encourage you to make a plan while you are thinking clearly, even in the pretense that maybe "the abuse won't happen again." Make it anyway, even if you never use it. This is the only way. When you survive the downside of the cycle, you are a wreck; you believe that it will never be good again, but you cannot function well enough to take all the necessary steps in planning and carrying out an escape. When you are on the upside, you believe that there is hope for the relationship, that he will not do it again. And so the cycle goes. I realize there is even more to face when you leave than when you stay in the relationship and tolerate the abuse. There is so much to face, and yet just surviving takes all your energy. There is not much left to plan an escape. But remember, there is help available. There are people who will stand with you. You are not alone.

I understand that your abuser may be throwing enough crumbs to keep the hope alive. A survivor from a concentration camp once wrote, "Where there is hope, there is life." He is trying to give you hope. He is trying to keep it alive. He will do all it takes to get you back. Then he'll do all it takes to drive you away. Then he'll do all it takes to get you back ... I read that in a pamphlet somewhere. It is real. It is like they have this psycho manual that instructs them on how to abuse, on how to break apart, to systematically destroy a person, and then put them back together just enough to let them breathe. But some days, I know, even breathing is hard. However, it will not change unless you, with God's help, change it. Reach up. Reach out ... before it is too late, and go.

I do not hate my abuser any longer. He is not the enemy; he is only a pawn in the enemy's hand. He is still bleeding from the wounds of his youth. Sometimes it is hard to separate the two, as still, so many years later he lashes out at me or attempts to restore what was lost without doing the healing work he needs to reconcile himself to God and himself, that would bring restoration. His brokenness flips that switch in his brain that causes him to retreat into old patterns and behaviors, bent on destruction for him and all those around him.

No, I do not hate him. I do have anger rise in me as I continue to hear the battle stories of other women still in it, see their scars being formed as I watch … see them waver, cave and fold back into their shells … fall back into what was, not realizing or believing what could be. It angers me as I see them go back and leave, time, and time again, to have a little more of their souls chopped away. That anger rises in me again as I hear them say, "But he says … but he wants … but he …" But the anger is not against those being victimized in an endless cycle of violence. No, it is not against them. My anger flares against the true enemy who steals our hearts and mind as he stamps his SILENCE on our souls. This anger is not dangerous to me. This anger ignites in me a passion to fight the battle for which God has been preparing me to fight; the battle to give voice to the plight of the voiceless ones and to set the captives free.

Appendix

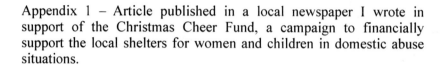

Appendix 1 – Article published in a local newspaper I wrote in support of the Christmas Cheer Fund, a campaign to financially support the local shelters for women and children in domestic abuse situations.

December 7, 2009

A Survivor of Domestic Violence

If I was a survivor of breast cancer, I could stand up, be seen, be heard in the battle and publicly proclaim my fight against it. But I am a survivor of domestic violence, so I can only fight in the war that wages underground. Our fight is a silent one, our plight a voiceless one. Sometimes we don't even know each other, for it is our own hidden secret. Yet we must remain silent to keep ourselves safe, and to give our children some semblance of normalcy, respect, and joy.

I lived in a volatile relationship for many years. Yet, I am an educated woman, who has a good career. I had no background of abuse in which I learned to be a victim. People who knew me before wondered how I could have let myself get into such a situation, or how I could have stayed so long. I wonder that myself sometimes. But it is such a complex issue that has as many different answers as there are women who are faced with domestic violence. We never really know how we will respond, or what we will actually do until we are put in the situation. I learned this the hard way. I'm just glad I had a chance to learn it at all.

Sometimes it is economical; where will I go, what will I do? But there is so much more to it than that. No, we do not like it. No, we are not addicted to the drama of it all. Far from it. I would give anything for the 'normal' calamities of this world to be a big deal in my life.

"If it were me …" you say, but by the time it has escalated to a dangerous level, physically or emotionally, you are NOT you. I was not me. That is the piece others do not understand unless you have walked through it. Entering into the relationship, you may be a strong, healthy woman, but by the time you recognize it for what it is, you are no longer that way. The abuser has slowly and methodically chipped away at your confidence, your relationships, your passions, your beliefs, your thoughts, your very identity. Your heart is left so bruised that it can shatter at anything, so you feel nothing, or there would be nothing left of you. The abuse does not start with a slap in the face, or even one of the "names in the book," all of which you will eventually be called. You would just walk away if that were so. No, it starts with a subtle comment that leaves you feeling a little off, a little unsettled. Then the manipulation and control tactics begin, making you start to doubt yourself, to question, to rationalize. The slow descent into madness continues with isolation; a little comment about your family or friends, about how they might not be what they seem … and so it begins. Intimidation and fear are soon established with covert, then overt and specific threats. Little by little the verbal assaults escalate until they become the mind numbing barrages that continue on into the middle of the night, and carry on for days. Until one day, the tension is gone, everything is swept under the rug, as if it never really happened, or if it did, it really wasn't as big a deal as you are making it out to be. Or sometimes the promises come, or the flowers, the gifts, the apologies, whatever it takes to get you back, to restore the hope and the dream, or to put you back together enough just to keep you breathing. But then it all happens again. And again. And again.

All your life energy and focus have shifted into your situation; about how you can stop what is happening and how it can even be real, as it does not seem logical or even possible. It makes absolutely no sense to you. So you try every logical solution to stop what is happening. But no matter what you try, how you "change the dance," it just gets worse, for they are not logical or rational, and therefore, the issue cannot be solved logically or rationally. Giving in means a period of relief, but the noose winds tighter, expectations higher, more restrictions. Standing up against it means instant escalation to dangerous levels. Still you fight. You think if you could work hard enough, phrase things a certain way, bring it up at the right time … just make him understand … try something different … anything … You don't want to give in … you don't want your children to have their family destroyed. (Though it already is, you just don't know it yet.)

And by this time, your mind has become so numbed by the shock and disbelief of the constant trauma, you barely have enough left inside of you to get through the day, to take care of your children, to even breathe, let alone to do all that it takes to get free.

So you draw the line in the sand, again, of what you will tolerate. "If he hits me, I'm gone," you say. But the first time wasn't a hit. It may be a slight push, a grab, or blocking your exit. Is it worth breaking apart the family, or putting your children through that huge ordeal and all of its repercussions over a little push? And so the line in the sand moves, little by little until your tolerance is so high, your perspective of what is normal so warped that what is horrific to others becomes somewhat normalized. You know it is not right, not healthy, but it is just the way it is. So you stay together for your children, not realizing the traumatic effects they are receiving by witnessing it, for you think you are hiding it, but you are not. It shows in your hollow eyes, your lifeless smile, in how you dare not answer the casual question "How are you?"

And finally, you do not have the strength to fight anymore. And so you give up all hope. Until one day, something snaps, or he does, and goes too far, and you realize that you did not break it, so you cannot fix it. You did not cause it, so no matter what you do, you cannot stop it. And you cannot take it anymore. It is not a way to live. It is not life. And so you leave. And you cry. And you heal. And you live. And you desperately want to help others get out, to start an underground railway that will provide the other captives with a way out. But you cannot. But I cannot. For now, I do not have the means, nor a way, so all I can do is remain anonymous, and give a little money to those who can help others like me. And so I do. And so I thank the staff at the shelters ... and the Christmas Cheer Fund for giving a voice to our silent cries.

Dedicated to all those still fighting:

Side by side, hand in hand, heart to heart; My Sisters my Friends

Appendix 2

(The story I had written during the seven month separation)

The little flower

One day, in the far corner of the garden, a little flower poked her head out of the soil. She stretched her leaves towards the sun and basked in its warmth. She thought, "What a nice little garden. I will like it here." And she proceeded to thrive and grow strong. And she was very, very happy.

Then one day, she heard a voice say, "What a pretty little flower. I will make it my own, and it will be the most beautiful flower in the garden." Now the flower, being the only flower in the back of the garden, was lonely at times, so she thought how wonderful it would be to have someone to take care of her needs and to give her so much attention.

So each day, the hands came and pulled the weeds out from around her, watered her, and told her how she was going to be the most beautiful flower in the garden. She stretched her face toward the sun, basked in its warmth, and beamed proudly. And she was very happy.

Then, one bright, sunny day, the voice snapped, "That petal is crooked. How can you be the most beautiful flower in the garden like this?" And the hands reached down and plucked out the petal. And the little flower cried, for it hurt terribly. But she bravely wiped away her tears and decided it must have been necessary, for the hands would never do anything to harm her. Then she reached her face toward the sun and basked in its warmth. And she was happy.

But each day, day after day, the voice found something else wrong with the little flower, and the hands reached down to extract it. And each day, day after day, the flower cried, and cried. She became weak and weary, and she hurt terribly, but still she reached her face up toward the sun, and it comforted her.

Then one day, the voice said, "I need to build a shed, in which I can keep all the tools, so I can take care of you properly." So, the hands built a shed right beside the flower, in which to keep the tools that would help tend to her needs. The little flower proudly stretched her face up to the sun, and basked in its warmth, knowing that soon she would be the most beautiful flower in the garden, and then everything would be okay. Soon the shed was finished, and filled with many, many tools. But the voice said, "It is not big enough. There are not enough tools. I will build another shed, and fill it with more tools. Then you will be the most beautiful flower in the garden. I will see to that." So the hands built another shed, right beside the flower. And the flower stretched up her neck proudly to face the sun, and basked in its warmth, but the sun's light was blocked out by the shed. And the flower was saddened.

And each day, the hands still came, and gave her water, and pulled off the offending pieces, but the voice was silent. Then one day, the voice screamed at the little flower, "How could you do this to me? Where did this weed come from? After everything I have done for you, you do this to me." And the foot came down and stepped on the little flower. Now the little flower, shook down to her roots, swore she did not know how it happened, and that she would not let it happen again. But in the days that followed, no matter how hard she tried, nor how much she cried, the weeds kept coming up around her. She could not stop them. And the voice grew angrier and angrier, and the hands stopped watering her. And some days, the foot would stomp on her. And the sun's light was still blocked out by the shed.

Then one day, the voice said, "I am doing this for your own good. It is sure to make you the most beautiful flower in the garden, you'll see." And the hands put the ugly metal fence around the little flower, to keep everything out--everything but the voice; the voice that haunted her, and the hands; the hands that hurt her, and the foot; the foot that crushed her into the ground. And now, the little flower could no longer see the beautiful flowers and trees in the distant gardens, the ones that had added some joy and color to her life, and had kept her from being so alone during the long, hard days in the far corner of the garden. And still, still there was no sunlight.

But one day the little flower, still shaking and trembling, realized that she did not want to be the most beautiful flower in the garden. She never had wanted to be the most beautiful flower in the garden. And she liked her petals, even if they were crooked. They were hers. So, the little flower began to slowly pull at her roots. Now, this was very painful, for her roots had grown deep, in search of the scarce water only found deep in the soil. And as she pulled, some of her roots broke off, and others were damaged. But, some of her roots remained intact and strong, and soon she was free. So, she jumped up out of the soil, jumped over the fence, and ran. She ran and ran, until she was back out into the sunlight, free from the fence, and the sheds, and the foot, and the hands, and the voice. Battered, and bruised, weak and weary, and missing many of her beautiful petals, she began her long journey, toward the distant garden, where she had seen, before the sheds and the fence, and the hands and the voice, all the other beautiful flowers and trees. And she was very, very frightened. But, she timidly reached her face up toward the sun, and she was comforted.

Appendix 3 (Sketches and notes from my journal)

I'm falling on my knees ... take the blackness away ... keep it from closing in on me!!!

There is a banquet for me ... it is all for me.

"This is all for you."

"God wants to take the grave clothes off. He wants you to lift your face towards Him."

*Psalm 34:5 - **those who look to him are radiant; their faces are never covered with shame**.*

~ you started something

~ why aren't you finishing it?

~ where are you now?

~why did you leave me?

A Final Word

My dear Reader,

God has put you so strongly in my heart. My heart aches for you and for all you are going through. Yet I have so much hope, trust, and faith that as you have put your heart out to Him, He has been healing your body, soul and spirit, and will continue to heal you, step by step. You will receive beauty for ashes in your life. God's Shekinah Glory will fill you with peace as you keep your heart open to Him and keep pouring out all that is ravaging you. I once was desperate and trapped. It was a journey, and it took time and work. But mostly it took finding the Father's heart in all of it. Through that, my own heart was touched.

I pray that your heart has been touched and that you have found some measure of peace and healing in the pages of my story ... of our story ...

... and maybe one day I will have the honor of meeting you, and you can tell me your story of victory and hope. Until then, walk with your head held high in the love of the Father ... Walk Tall. I will walk with you.

♥ Love in Christ,

Calli J. Linwood

For the glory of God

End Notes

Bancroft, Lundy. Why Does He Do That? Inside the Minds of Angry and Controlling Men. New York: Berkley Books, 2003.

Carothers, Merlin. Power in Praise. Escondido: Merlin R. Carothers, 1972.

Cooke, Graham. Living Your Truest Identity. Vancouver: Brilliant Book House, 2012

Evans, Patricia. Verbal Abuse Survivors Speak Out. Avon: Adams Media Corporation, 2003

Meyer, Joyce. Beauty for Ashes. Nashville: Faith Words, 2003.

Coming Soon ...

Break Forth

Calli J. Linwood

I collapsed to the floor in my classroom, my legs unable to hold me up any longer. In tears, I tried to wrap my mind around the reality that I might no longer be able to keep teaching, or do anything else, for that matter. I had taught for 20 years ... and as a single parent, it was my family's sole means of support. My doctor told me to get my papers in order in the likely case that I would have to go on disability. I recognized how close I had come to being mentally and emotionally broken almost beyond repair, but I had no idea the toll it had taken on my body. It was just now starting to show up ... now, after I finally had gotten back up on my feet mentally, emotionally and spiritually.

"Lord!" I cried." "My spring is supposed to be here! I have worked so hard and healed so much ... why is this happening now? I already have a story! I don't need another one!"

"Calli, my dear, it is not another story ... it is the same story ... just another chapter ..."

CPSIA information can be obtained at www.ICGtesting.com
Printed in the USA
LVOW07s2223271115

464423LV00008B/13/P